THE EVERYTHING

GUIDE TO STUDY SKILLS

Dear Reader,

Each student approaches school differently. Some arrive at school wide-eyed and overwhelmed. Others are highly motivated and ready to tackle all problems, academic and social. The vast majority of students fall between these two extremes. Whoever you are, *The Everything® Guide to Study Skills* will help you be the best student *you* can be.

The ideas within are culled from my work with hundreds of students across the spectrum, from the least motivated to the highly driven. My expertise comes as a result of my careers as an assistant director of college admission, test prep instructor, high school teacher, private college counselor, and lifelong passionate student. I have my finger on the pulse of what students in the twenty-first century experience academically, socially, and in extracurricular activities. But let me emphasize what I feel is most important in the educational process: **What you get out of studying depends on what you put into it.**

Making the effort to be a good student is worth it—and not just because you improve your chances of earning high grades. The skills you develop as a student—approaching problems strategically and intelligently, communicating clearly and efficiently, and applying what you know to new situations—will be useful after school as well. Though it may be tough to believe now, learning can be an exciting and enriching experience that you enjoy your entire life!

Enjoy using this guide on your journey to become a more successful student and learner. Good luck!

Cindy Clumeck Muchnick, MA

www.cynthiamuchnick.com

Welcome to the EVERYTHING. Series!

These handy, accessible books give you all you need to tackle a difficult project, gain a new hobby, comprehend a fascinating topic, prepare for an exam, or even brush up on something you learned back in school but have since forgotten.

You can choose to read an *Everything®* book from cover to cover or just pick out the information you want from our five useful boxes: e-questions, e-facts, e-alerts, e-ssentials, and e-quotes. We give you everything you need to know on the subject, but throw in a lot of fun stuff along the way, too.

We now have more than 400 *Everything®* books in print, spanning such wide-ranging categories as weddings, pregnancy, cooking, music instruction, foreign language, crafts, pets, New Age, and so much more. When you're done reading them all, you can finally say you know *Everything®*!

QUESTION
Answers to common questions

FACT
Important snippets of information

ALERT
Urgent warnings

ESSENTIAL
Quick handy tips

QUOTE
Words of wisdom from experts in the field

PUBLISHER Karen Cooper

DIRECTOR OF ACQUISITIONS AND INNOVATION Paula Munier

MANAGING EDITOR, EVERYTHING® SERIES Lisa Laing

COPY CHIEF Casey Ebert

ASSISTANT PRODUCTION EDITOR Jacob Erickson

ACQUISITIONS EDITOR Lisa Laing

SENIOR DEVELOPMENT EDITOR Brett Palana-Shanahan

ASSOCIATE DEVELOPMENT EDITOR Hillary Thompson

EDITORIAL ASSISTANT Ross Weisman

EVERYTHING® SERIES COVER DESIGNER Erin Alexander

LAYOUT DESIGNERS Colleen Cunningham, Elisabeth Lariviere, Ashley Vierra, Denise Wallace

Visit the entire Everything® series at *www.everything.com*

THE
EVERYTHING®
GUIDE TO
STUDY SKILLS

Strategies, tips, and tools you need
to succeed in school!

Cynthia Clumeck Muchnick, MA

Aadamsmedia
Avon, Massachusetts

To Justin, Jacob, Ross, and Alexa, who teach me every day. And to Adam for sharing this adventure as my husband, teammate, cheerleader, and best friend.

An Everything® Series Book.
Everything® and everything.com® are registered trademarks of F+W Media, Inc.

Published by Adams Media, a division of F+W Media, Inc.
57 Littlefield Street, Avon, MA 02322 U.S.A.
www.adamsmedia.com

Contains material adapted from *The Everything® Study Book* by Steven Frank, copyright
© 1997 by F+W Media, Inc., ISBN 10: 1- 55850-615-2, ISBN 13: 978-1-55850-615-2.

ISBN 10: 1-4405-0744-9
ISBN 13: 978-1-4405-0744-1
eISBN 10: 1-4405-0745-7
eISBN 13: 978-1-4405-0745-8

Printed in the United States of America.

10 9 8 7 6 5 4 3

Library of Congress Cataloging-in-Publication Data
Muchnick, Cynthia Clumeck.
The everything guide to study skills / Cynthia Clumeck Muchnick.
   p. cm.
Includes bibliographical references and index.
ISBN 978-1-4405-0744-1 (alk. paper)
1. Study skills. I. Title.
LB1049.M83 2011
371.3028'1—dc22
2011010227

This book is available at quantity discounts for bulk purchases.
For information, please call 1-800-289-0963.

Contents

Acknowledgments

This book could not have been possible without the support of many people in my life. Thanks to my literary agent, Grace Freedson, for your help, persistence, and belief in my project. You found my book a home and a way to share my knowledge and passion with an audience and readership. Thank you to my publisher Adams Media and especially Lisa Laing for her patience and for wanting me, and Brett Palana-Shanahan for helping my words come together into the unique *Everything*® brand. To Vicky deFelice, my friend, colleague, mentor, and constant resource. To my son's favorite English and literature teacher, Brian Rogers, who willingly took the time when he barely knew me to consult on my chapters on writing. Finally, to the many NACAC listserv members for being my virtual colleagues throughout the years.

Thanks to my parents, Gloria and Jack Clumeck, who always encouraged me to make lemonade from lemons and who appreciate my true essence and enthusiasm for life in constant motion. To my sisters, Karen Shea and Linda Rosen, for letting me practice my expertise on their kids and for respecting and valuing my advice and insights. To Sherri, Ron, Kim, and Marc Muchnick for your continued support and assistance with my online learning chapter. To my special girlfriends who appreciate and understand me in my chaotic world: Cynthia "you complete me" Jenkins, Nancy Cutler-Dye, Mollie Hudner-Thompson, Kiko Mitchell, Robindira Unsworth, and Christina Welford. To women and teachers I devotedly admire and respect: Robin Preiss-Glasser, Debbie Deener, Nancy Chase, and my all-time favorite Stanford Professor Jody Maxmin. Thank you nanny extraordinaire, Jackie Powell, for tirelessly helping me with my four children so I could find time to write this book in between naps, work, and carpooling. You have saved me more times than you will ever know. Thank you Justin, Jacob, Ross, and Ally for filling me with pride and joy each day. To Adam, for your unwavering love, support, and belief in me always. This journey together just keeps getting better.

And finally, to all of my students and parents who through the years have entrusted me to guide you through this often stress-filled, anxiety-ridden process of navigating high school and college admission. I feel valued to be your consultant and share my expertise. I genuinely love what I do!

The Top Ten Habits of
Successful Students

1. Treat school as your job.

2. Pursue learning with passion, vigor, and an open mind.

3. Always attend class. Arrive on time and ready to learn.

4. Do your homework and extra credit options!

5. Set academic, extracurricular, and social goals and aim to achieve them.

6. Become an active learner, a good listener, and class participant. Think outside the box and strive to make interdisciplinary connections among your various classes.

7. Demonstrate responsibility and take ownership of your education. Don't be afraid to take risks and learn from your mistakes.

8. Master and refine your ability to schedule, manage your time, and be organized.

9. Develop your writing skills.

10. Build relationships with your teachers. Attend office hours outside of class whenever possible.

Introduction

IT MAY SEEM FROM the outside as though learning comes easy for the high-achievers who get great grades. You know who they are—the class "brainiacs," the award winners, the straight-A students, the ones the teacher calls on most in class. The fact is, many of those high-achievers are just pre-wired to perform and practice many of the techniques contained in this book!

Don't get *too* caught up in trying to match those straight-A students, though. Sometimes a "B" is the best you are capable of earning. If so, bravo for that "B"! Success is being the best student *you in particular* can be and achieving the highest grades you're capable of achieving by following that age-old adage: "Just do your best."

Sometimes it takes an academic slump to get you motivated to make a change. Sometimes motivation comes from an anxiety pushing you to make your family, teachers, or peers proud of you. But you should also read this book to improve because *you* want to.

You might already use some of the ideas suggested here. If so, keep up the good work. If not, try a few and you will likely achieve results right away. Remember, as a student you get to reinvent yourself each and every day socially and academically; you can decide to wake up tomorrow and implement some of these practical suggestions. Also, check out the "E-Quotes" in each chapter to read how actual students are applying these ideas and finding success.

As you already know and will learn more and more, academic performance and choices you make in school directly impact the possibility of attending the college or graduate schools you want. Beyond that, all of the suggestions of this book can be further applied to life experiences outside the classroom and in the workplace as well.

Do you need to be a straight-A student to benefit from the ideas contained in *The Everything® Guide to Study Skills*? Absolutely not. In fact, these strategies give average students the "secrets" that many high-achievers already put into practice. These ideas will help you reduce the stress of school by offering easy-to-digest, doable tips that you can put into practice right away. You will enjoy tangible rewards from your dedication in the form of improved academic and effort grades.

CHAPTER 1

School Is Your Job

Most adults wake up each morning, get dressed, grab breakfast or coffee, and race out the door to work so they can provide for their families. Well, guess what? You have a job, too: School. Your job is to be the best student you can be. And it isn't always easy. So how can you do your job really well? Just like a "regular" employee: showing up on time, working hard to impress the boss, being nice and pleasant at work, being a team player, demonstrating leadership, and through community involvement or volunteer work. How do people get promoted and attain positive job recognition from bosses? They work hard by committing to doing the best job possible. You can be successful at school with the same method!

Pleasing the "Boss"

More specifically, your job in school is to work as hard as you can and perform to the best of your ability for your bosses—your teachers. Here's where it gets tricky: Unlike most employees, who probably report to one boss or supervisor (or maybe they are even lucky enough to be their own boss), you have six to eight bosses to please: all of your various teachers. And here's the even trickier part. You have to figure out *what* she wants, *how* she wants it, *when* she wants it, and then give it to her exactly *that* way. That's what you have to do—even if the assignment isn't fun; even if the subject is not your favorite; and even if you don't respect the teacher. **Figure out what your teachers want, how they want it, and when they want it. Then give it to them that way.**

It's easy to complain about teachers. Maybe you feel a particular teacher doesn't like you. Maybe you got the super-hard teacher who never gives As. Maybe you have the teacher who didn't like your older sibling, so now he has a preconception in his mind of who you are. Or maybe you have the cranky old teacher who makes you memorize and regurgitate everything she says and then never tests you on it? Well, just as you might not like everyone in the workplace or even in life for that matter, you may not like all of your teachers. But, even if you don't like them or their subject matter, you still have to try hard to do your best. In school as in real life, you have to bite the bullet sometimes and perform the way your boss wants you to perform even if it is uncomfortable or not the way you like to do it.

ALERT

Don't burn bridges with your teachers or end a course on a bad note. There is always the possibility you will come across this teacher again in a future class or activity. Better to instead try to reach an understanding than to be unnecessarily argumentative or challenging.

Think of tough teachers like an extra challenge you can work hard to overcome. If you put your mind to it, you can prove to him you *can* do it *his* way. You will likely gain the teacher's respect—and you may even figure out why the particular teacher prefers a certain testing style or teaching method. If you're struggling to understand why your teacher makes you memorize vocabulary words for a quiz every Friday, for example, ask him privately after class what that method accomplishes. Maybe over his years of experience, he's found that's the best way for students to remember the new words. There's nothing wrong with asking a teacher questions like that as long as you approach him nicely, with respect and an open mind.

Here are some strategies and steps to take to show your teacher that you respect him and are willing to learn in the style he prefers:

- Introduce yourself to the teacher after class.
- Arrive on time.
- Arrive with the assigned textbooks and possible summer work that was preassigned.
- Sit close to the front of the room.
- Sit up straight and be attentive—no cell phones, doodling, or staring out the window.
- Be engaged in class and have your voice heard when appropriate.
- Demonstrate to your teacher you really understand that material by making connections beyond the lecture, readings, or presentation. For example, link an idea to another class or concept to show you are making relevant connections among your coursework.
- Take notes, listen well, and maintain eye contact as much as possible.
- Dress tastefully to make a good first impression.
- Ask a question or make a comment to have your voice heard the first day (or week) of class.
- Say hello to your teacher outside of class.
- Attend the first office hours offered (or the first few) even if you don't need any help. Just go and make some casual conversation or bring a factoid, question, or tidbit to get on your teacher's radar screen.
- Thank your teacher at the end of class. (You can do it in private if you feel embarrassed in front of other students!) Remember, teachers are working hard for you.

Get in the habit of practicing these steps and they will just become second nature. Building a good rapport with your teacher never hurts. These strategies apply not only to your classroom but also to life beyond school in dealing with future bosses, advisors, or adult friends of your parents who can also be great resources to you in the job world. "What a nice young person," you'd like them to say or think, referring to your impressive people skills and presentation. Your teacher will appreciate your efforts.

Following the Boss's Instructions

Your boss, the teacher, will give you some obvious clues on how to please her. The first is the syllabus. That's just a fancy way of describing a handout usually given out on the first day of class, posted online, or both. It is an outline or template of what you can expect for the semester or year. Read and study it closely and be sure you understand what is required of you to succeed in this class.

A syllabus usually includes the following information:

- **Class Information**: Teacher name, contact information, office hours, office and course location and number, and other pertinent course information.
- **Course Description**: Sometimes taken from a course catalog or prepared by the teacher to summarize the content and scope of what will be taught during the term.
- **Course Objectives**: What the teacher hopes you will gain from this class; goals the teacher has set for students to meet.
- **Texts and Supplies**: A listing of the textbooks or online materials required for the class as well as any special supplies you will need to complete the course (such as a scientific calculator, three-section divided spiral notebook, or compass).
- **The Grading Structure**: Typically this section is broken down into percentages of how the class will be weighted among attendance, homework, essays, quizzes, tests, final exam, and participation.
- **Classroom Rules**: Such as no cell phones, whether laptops are allowed, etc.

Sometimes a syllabus is distributed on the first day of class with additional verbal instructions from the teacher, so listen closely. You may learn information from your teacher beyond what is written in the syllabus. You will witness your teacher's style and hear expectations.

For example, let's say your boss for Introduction to Art History stresses that he values the importance of remembering the names and dates of important pieces of art. Now you know what he wants: memorization. Make a stack of flash cards for yourself with a picture of the piece of art and its name and artist, or highlight your class notes or textbook and memorize away. Or, perhaps your philosophy teacher tells you his class will be in a lecture format and that you will be quizzed exclusively on what he tells you in lectures. He then explains that your textbook and homework assignments are mainly for supplemental background information but still need to be read and turned in. Now you know to pay extra-close attention to the lectures.

ESSENTIAL

Ask upperclassmen about the reputation and expectations of your teachers. They are the most recent "employees" of this boss, and they usually have strong opinions and great insight.

An English teacher may base a large percentage of your grade on class participation; if so, come prepared and be sure your voice is heard at least a few times a week in his class and check in at office hours from time to time. Your history teacher may say that he wants to hear your *original* thoughts regarding the lecture or reading assignment. If so, have some ideas ready to share in class, or at minimum think on your feet during a lecture so you can ask a question or voice a comment. Yes, it is tricky to get to know exactly what each teacher wants from you, but the syllabus combined with the teacher's first day of class presentation will give you many clues on how to succeed in each class.

QUESTION

Do I have to agree with everything my teachers tell me or even believe everything they say in class?
No. But you do have to do it *their* way because *they* are the bosses. Ultimately, you need to please the boss to gain that promotion in the form of a good grade or good participation.

Figuring out what each teacher wants can actually be a fun and challenging task. Does your teacher always check homework? Do it *every* time. Does he speak or pay closer attention to the kids who sit in the front rows? Sit in the front! Or request to have your assigned seat moved there. Does your teacher mention her office hours weekly? Then schedule it and go. Does your teacher encourage e-mail correspondence and questions outside of class? Be sure to communicate your questions in that manner. Repeat the mantra: **Figure out what your teachers want, how they want it, and when they want it. Then give it to them that way.**

The First Day on the Job

Just like any other situation when you meet someone, you want to make a good first impression when you meet your teacher or professor for the first time. Know that your teacher is also making a first impression the first day of class. He is trying to get across his message, his expectations of the course, and your role in it, and to introduce his personality and teaching style to you. Pay close attention to these verbal cues and take note. Do your homework from the get-go to stay on top of the coursework so you don't fall behind.

FACT

Eating a healthy breakfast and getting a good night's sleep makes a big difference in your alertness in class, attention span, and absorption of material. Be sure to eat and sleep well, just like mom used to tell you.

If there is time after class (if not, try office hours), introduce yourself to your teacher so she can put a face with a name. In the future, if you need to e-mail or meet with her again you can remind her you were the student who introduced yourself or asked a certain question during class.

Don't introduce yourself to teachers just as they arrive to the room or right before class, as usually they are trying to get everyone settled down and organize their materials. The end of class is a more relaxed and natural time, assuming they are not running off to another class.

Networking with Classmates

Friends, older siblings, and upperclassmen can be your best resources in school for many reasons. Since they have "been there," many upperclassmen can give you the lowdown on teachers and what they expect. Seek advice and ask questions of those ahead of you. Older students feel proud to be asked their opinion by younger students. In the realm of confusing teenage social dynamics, that recognition matters. Don't be shy. Be aware that asking five students will elicit five different answers, and your solution or answer is probably in pieces of those answers.

Do your homework on upcoming teachers by researching in advance of the first day of class from older students who have had them before. You will usually get an earful of anecdotes, information on how a teacher grades and what they like in a student. Luckily, students love to share their opinions and tell it like it is: the good, the bad, and the ugly. It's a good idea to seek students of a similar academic level to you to hear about an experience that will likely be the same as yours.

Seeking words of wisdom from those who have "been there and survived" can make you feel "not alone" in your experience. Plus, you can get great tips and nuggets of information on how to win over a teacher, what projects are the most important to ace, and strategies for surviving the class. Who knows? An upperclassman may also be a great person to ask to serve as a tutor or peer advisor for you if you are struggling your way through a class.

Questions to Ask Upperclassmen

Below is a list of suggested questions to ask upperclassmen on bus rides home from games, at lunch, in the parking lot before or after school, or in your dorm.

- What has been your favorite/least favorite class in the school?
- Who do you think is the best/worst teacher in the school?
- What campus tradition do you enjoy the most?
- What types of clubs/sports/groups/etc. do you participate in?
- Who is the hardest teacher but the one you learn from the most?
- What activity should I avoid at school?
- Where are you applying to college or graduate school?

Try asking any of these questions as icebreakers to get your conversation started with someone you did not previously know.

Networking with Your Peers

Finally, think of your current classmates as co-workers. Learn which ones are strong students or class leaders—you might want to consider partnering up with them on group projects. You can learn a great deal from your peers and model yourself after them if they have already demonstrated success in a class, have gained a strong academic reputation, or appear to be on good terms with the teacher.

ESSENTIAL

Try to set up study groups or partners in at least the subjects that don't come as easily to you. If you work with classmates, your brain will be more engaged. How so? Communicating material to others uses many parts of your brain and stimulates you to learn and make connections more than if you study by yourself.

Getting Promoted

Teachers serve as great sounding boards to recommend what class you should take next. They often know what their colleagues' classes are like and if you would be a good fit for another course, perhaps one that logically follows the class you've just taken. Obviously, the better you have gotten to know your teacher through the course of your term, the more comfortable you will be asking them for their thoughts on what to take next. Also, if you are a borderline student who is uncertain if you should continue to an honors, Advanced Placement, or seminar level of a class, sometimes you need both a strong grade in the preliminary class *and* a recommendation from your previous teacher. So, be sure they know who you are!

Additionally, at the conclusion of each class, think about how the strength of your relationship with your teacher could help you in your next academic endeavor. Every teacher is a potential recommender for a summer program, college application, or graduate program. Teachers are willing to write recommendations for the students they know best and who perform with consistent effort for them, regardless of the grade they receive. Your teachers want to know you before they write about you, however, so the more substantial your relationship, the more insightful the recommendation will be.

ALERT

Studies show that having poor or nonexistent relationships with teachers is a primary reason students drop out of school. That's another good reason to build those relationships whenever possible!

Be Your Own Boss

Even though you may feel you have very little choice in the matter when it comes to classes, teachers, or your school career for that matter, you do. You are in charge of your job because everything you do is your choice. That is what the school experience can really be summed up as: *your choices.* You choose when you want to study or not (even if your parents nag you!). You choose whether to play video games or spend the extra time memorizing your Spanish vocabulary words for tomorrow's quiz. You choose to text and instant message your friends until all hours of the night or review those flash cards one last time and get some sleep so you are fresh for a quiz in the morning. When you think about things that way, you can see how you have more control over your school experience than you may realize.

Some expert advice: Choose wisely. The choices you make *do* count and make a difference. Admission officers consider everything you have done with your time academically and outside of school since the summer after eighth grade (when you technically are a high school student and primary school graduate). So, it *all* counts. And it is all *your* choice. The better your choices, the more options you will have later when it comes to colleges. Will you make mistakes? Absolutely. Oftentimes those mistakes not only make for the greatest learning experiences and build character, but also they serve as terrific nuggets for college essays when it comes time to fill out your applications.

QUOTE

"During the first weeks of school and each new semester, I pay special attention to my teacher's class expectations. I study the syllabus closely and immediately write office hours into my schedule, treating them as though they are an additional class. I use office hours in case I need extra review of concepts that challenge me, have a poor test or paper grade, or just want to say hello and strike up a conversation."

—Sara F., Sophomore

CHAPTER 2

Getting the Most Out of Classroom Time

You primarily learn within the four walls of your classroom. Books, supplemental materials, and the Internet only teach content. The information teachers share in their classroom—the human element of communicating and transmitting information to students—serves as the foundation for your education. Being a productive, prepared student in any classroom, from the smallest seminar to the largest lecture hall, is crucial in being able to achieve success in school. What you learn in the classroom should carry beyond its walls and into your life outside. Making connections between the classroom and outside world demonstrates that you value and apply your education to life.

Where to Sit

If you attend a small private school that offers many small classes or seminars with under twenty students, this step may be extremely simple for you since you are already sitting in close proximity to your boss—er, teacher. But for the majority of you who are in larger classes, this task can be more difficult to accomplish.

Why You Should Sit Up Front

You should sit in one of the first three rows of every class. Why is sitting up front so important? Proximity to your teacher is crucial. The boss is up front, looking out and teaching to a classroom full of faces. The faces often blur together from class to class, especially if your teacher teaches multiple courses to multiple grades. So how can you be certain to be recognized and appreciated as an individual employee—er, student? By sitting close to the boss. While it may seem to you as though your teachers know you very well, remember that you are one of at least one hundred or several hundred students they teach throughout the course of the day. Be sure they really do know you. Sitting up close just makes that easier for them.

If you select a seat in the first three rows, you will also be less tempted to doze off, pass notes, check your text messages, or goof around. Physical closeness to your teachers is a key to them "knowing" you better as a student. You will probably be called on more, and that will force you to be better prepared and will serve as an incentive for you to perform well in that class. Sit up straight. Be focused and serious about your job. What is your job again? Absorbing, assimilating, and learning the material that is being presented to you. Take notes, listen well, and maintain eye contact as much as possible.

In addition, studies show that from the vantage point of the front of a classroom or audience, a speaker's eyes scan the room in the form of a reverse capital letter "T." That means the front row(s) and everyone down the middle receives the most eye contact from the teacher. Those sitting on the edge of the room, along the wall aisles or in the back rows tend to get overlooked. So, if you cannot find a way to get up front, then be sure you are sitting in the middle of the classroom.

Be sure you use good posture when you are in class. Slumping in your chair or putting your feet up against the chair in front of you can make you sleepy and less alert. Poor posture also sends a message to your teacher indicating you are disengaged from the presentation.

As the teacher speaks, he moves his eyes back and forth, scanning the classroom. If his eyes come across you and you are looking back at your teacher, or even nodding or smiling, then his subliminal perception of you is, "Oh, good. Joe's alert and paying close attention." No matter how boring the topic is to you or how sleepy or hungry you are, pay attention.

How to Change Your Seat

What if you're assigned a seat alphabetically and your last name starts with "Z" so you're assigned to the back row in certain classes? Simply come up with a reason to request that you sit closer forward. How about:

- "I am having trouble hearing from the back row. Can I please move my seat closer up? I don't mind sitting in the aisle along the wall."
- "I'm having trouble seeing the board from the back." If you have glasses or contacts that is a bonus!
- "Are you willing to shift seats when the next term/semester begins? I'd like to sit up closer to feel more connected to what is going on."
- "Is it okay if I found someone in the front who doesn't mind switching seats so I can sit closer to the front?"
- "I focus better in class when I sit further forward. Is there any way I can move up to get closer to the front rows?"

If you are lucky enough to be in a classroom that has desks arranged in a circle or chairs around one large table or Harkness table (where the teacher sits at a round table with you) then, guess what? *Everyone* has a front-row seat and you are fortunate to be in a class that is conducive to dialogue, participation, and group interaction. A circular arrangement also helps you avoid hiding from your teacher; by definition you have to be actively engaged and alert.

And, by the way, don't worry if your classmates call you a "kiss up." While you don't want to become unlikeable in their estimation, take a step back and realize that your reputation in school does not live with you forever; and if you really network well you will be well-liked by both your fellow students and your teachers. You are your own advocate, and school success is defined by the choices *you* make. And these choices *you* make *do* impact the options you will have in the future regarding college and career choices. So make the choice to sit in a position that gives you the best chance at success.

What if none of your attempts work to get you moved up closer? Be sure to visit that teacher in office hours more often or introduce yourself after class, expressing your desire to move closer if and when a seat becomes available. Don't give up on your quest!

What to Bring

Other than the obvious bookbag, notebook, pencil, pen, highlighter, sticky notes, homework, and books for the class, you may also choose to bring a laptop for taking notes. You'll also want to bring an assignment book or calendar to organize homework and project due dates, test and quiz dates, and long-term assignment deadlines.

Classrooms or lecture halls can be too hot or too cold depending on the season or the number of people in a lecture hall. It is always a good idea to dress in layers so you can adjust your own temperature as necessary. A mini book light (inexpensive and available at all bookstores) can also be helpful to have on hand in courses where the room is darkened for slides or projected images, such as art history or film classes.

ESSENTIAL

Bring a water bottle to class in case you get thirsty—it will save you from leaving class to get a drink and can act as a helpful pick-me-up if you are feeling fatigued or sluggish. Don't drink too much, though, or you may waste your precious class time in the bathroom!

Other than bringing physical items, do not forget to bring your positive attitude and mindset, which should be one that is seeking clues and taking in information, questioning, and being thoughtful about the subject matter. Regardless of how much you like or dislike a class or teacher, adopt the attitude that each class offers a new challenge to overcome or topic to investigate and examine, and you can hone listening and note-taking skills each day. Come to class prepared, and don't become one of those annoying students who borrows a pen and paper each week from someone different. Have a notebook or binder dedicated to each class, and always bring it with you.

Avoiding Distractions and Pitfalls

Avoid distracting people at all costs while doing your job. Try not to sit next to the cute guy you have a crush on, or your best friend, or anyone with whom you may be tempted to talk, socialize, or flirt. Some students are noisy in the classroom; fidgeting is part of their nature. Gum chewers, frequent texters, or even those with laptops can distract you from your job of being a successful student. Be aware of those classmates and avoid sitting near them.

Turn off your cell phone—not just to vibrate but to silence or off altogether. Put all other tempting electronics away out of sight, deep in your school bag or locker. Wear a watch so you don't have to turn to look at a classroom wall clock. This may not seem like a big deal, but a teacher can misinterpret your curiosity about the time as boredom or disrespect. Instead of blurting out questions when they pop into your head, jot down possible questions to ask in the margins of your notes to ask when the time is appropriate. Use your pen or pencil to take note of interesting observations or connections you have made during a lecture or reading that you can bring up in class if there is an opportunity.

ALERT

Double- and triple-check that you have turned off your cell phone. Teachers have been known to kick students out of class or throw phones in the trashcan if a ringer or buzzing noise interrupts class.

Here are some other rules to avoid potential distractions:

- Don't pass notes.
- Don't check texts or e-mails.
- Don't bring in the sports pages or surf the Internet.
- Don't come to class hungry so your stomach growls loudly for all to hear.

If you avoid these distractions and temptations, you'll come to class prepared to be engaged and participate.

Do Your Homework!

Don't forget, if you don't turn in an assignment or you miss a day of school and don't take the initiative to make up the work, you will risk receiving a zero in the grade book. Those zeros add up and average into your final grade. A zero on a missed assignment can even go so far as to ruin your grade. So stay on top of what you need to do and build up that extra cushion for yourself through extra credit points.

Many schools allow up to 3 percent of a grade increase (or one grade increment from a B+ to an A– for example) for earned extra credit, so those extra points can certainly add up to an improved grade when your grade is on the cusp.

The same goes for homework. The most basic rule to passing and being successful in any class is to do your homework. Homework serves as the basic foundation of what you need to do to succeed in your job as a student. It represents the *minimum* expected of you, so be sure you *always* do it. Again, homework assignments may contribute towards your final grade, but they also let you and your teacher know areas you need to work on and better understand.

Always Do Extra Credit

Who says nothing in life is free? The best-kept secret in school is extra credit. When it comes to extra credit, do it! Find out how the extra credit or home-work points contribute to your final grade so you can remind yourself of how important it is. Any time a teacher offers extra credit, they are seeking answers to a few of these questions:

- Who can figure out this extra-tough problem?
- Who is willing to go beyond the call of duty and do a bit more work on top of what is assigned?
- Who is planning ahead and wants to maximize his chances of having a great grade in my class by securing a safety net of sorts, just in case he doesn't do as well as he wants on a paper or final exam? Or, who wants to put a few extra points accumulated in the GPA bank?

What's wrong with being the student who is the answer to any of those questions or assumptions? Nothing.

Think of extra credit as free money. It's out there for you to take and keep. And here's the greatest secret of all. If you do the extra credit and get it wrong—even if you miss every part of the assignment either once or every time, you are no worse off than before you attempted it.

In fact, you are even a bit *better* off in the eyes of your teacher, since he or she sees that you are putting extra effort into their class even if what is being asked is stumping you. Teachers *like* students who put in effort, and when it comes time to hand out grades at the end of the term, they *do* glance at that grade book and see who has been doing the extra credit; whether you earn all of the points offered for it is another story. Just *doing* it does help you.

ALERT

Being stressed can impact your attitude and schoolwork. Make sure to practice some form of stress reduction each day and to "turn off your brain" to release it from stress and academic thoughts. Yoga, breathing exercises, jogging, or just going for a walk in the fresh air can calm your mind and body when you feel tense.

And, if extra credit is not offered in a class, ask for it! If you are falling behind, are in a slump, or are having difficulty maintaining a good grade in a class, ask the teacher if there is any extra credit you can do. A teacher might consider giving some to you if you ask even if she is not giving it to the whole class.

Also, believe it or not, extra credit can be fun. Think if it as high-level "learning for learning's sake." What have you got to lose except your time? And for that time spent, you may gain some points you would not have earned otherwise, and a nod of approval and respect from your teacher. Find out how the extra credit points break down at your school or in your particular class so you can calculate how much this "free money" will help you.

Electronics and the Classroom

The kinds of technology available to students and teachers these days is astounding. It can enhance your learning experience by exposing you to engaging multimedia presentations, top-notch experts around the world, and a plethora of research and data. Technology can also be distracting and a nuisance if it's not used properly, however. Make sure you're using each piece in the way your teacher prefers so you can maximize your learning experience. Here are a few tips.

Using a Laptop

Many students and even teachers have begun to bring laptop computers to class. While this might seem like a good idea, it's not really recommended for several reasons, including:

- Most people write by hand more quickly than they type.
- Typing on a laptop can distract your fellow students and, worse, your instructor.
- Writing by hand gives you greater flexibility. You can also draw signs, and use arrows and symbols more easily by hand.

As you will soon see, you'll be working a great deal with the notes you take in class, making additions and revisions. It's easier to do this on paper than on the computer. If you want to keep your notes on your computer, you can always type them when you get home. In fact, this process is a good way to help you rethink and reorganize your notes, and it will help you remember them.

Other Media Your Teacher Might Use

Rather than using your own electronic devices, why not instead admire the Smart Board in your classroom (if your teacher is fortunate enough to have one) or enjoy a PowerPoint presentation if one is given? Perhaps your teacher is media-savvy and current in the use of interactive technology in his presentations. Some teachers even incorporate streaming video from YouTube into their lectures or use Skype to communicate and teleconference with classrooms across the world. Video images or music can assist a teacher in illustrating something in a lesson.

Some teachers have begun to find benefits in social networks such as Facebook, where they can create closed groups to interact and disseminate information to their students. Other teachers post blogs or conduct podcasts for their students.

The bottom line: leave your personal technology behind when attending class, but take full advantage of whatever technology your teacher offers to enhance his lesson.

Leave the Recorder at Home

Some students think they'll take the easy way out by bringing a handheld recording device to class and rely on that instead of taking notes. The recorder ultimately means much more work than you may realize, however. You will get home and have all that recorded information to review, which means, in effect, going to class twice.

By taking notes in class instead, you're already beginning to digest and to edit the information. For example, you might not write down information that you already know or have taken notes on previously. You also don't need to write down the detailed explanations your professor makes to recall and understand a particular concept. Since your notes are succinct, they will take far less time to read over than it would take to listen to a recorded lecture again.

Then there's the problem of mechanical difficulties. What if the batteries run out or the teacher's voice is too low or muffled? What if you accidentally delete your recording? Minimize these risks by leaving the recorder at home.

That said, there is one way that electronic recording may help you. If you must miss a lecture for some reason, you might want to have a friend record it so you'll be able to keep up. (Be sure this request is okay with the teacher first.) Make certain, though, that you listen to the lecture and take notes just as if you were sitting in class.

Strategies for Effective Listening

We take it for granted that we all know how to listen, that listening is a natural skill requiring no work at all. The truth is, listening is a difficult task and very few people know how to do it well. Have you ever been in the midst of a conversation with someone, nodding your head in agreement, and suddenly found yourself unable to respond to a question they've just asked? While you may have technically heard him, you weren't *listening* to him. How about when someone tells you his name and within moments you have forgotten it?

Why is listening so difficult? One reason is that students and adults confuse *hearing* with *listening*. Hearing is *passive*; it means some sound has reverberated in your ear, whether or not you wanted it to, and there's been a noise. Listening, on the other hand, is an *active* process. It implies that you must *do* something to accomplish it. It takes action and, often, work to listen well. For example, let's say you are sitting on a crowded train talking with a friend. You hear the noise of the train, the chatter of passengers around you, the iPod echoes blasted by a kid next to you and, somewhere in all that, you even hear your friend. But to understand what your friend is telling you, you need to *do* something; you need to listen to distinguish her words from all the background noise.

The same principle applies to classroom lectures. There may not be the same amount of noise in a lecture room as on a crowded train (although there is plenty of distracting racket, from feet shuffling to coughing to heaters or air conditioners blowing), but you still have to work hard to listen to the professor's words. The following strategies will help you learn effective listening. They can help with your note-taking as well as with any interpersonal encounters, from conversations to job interviews. Develop good listening skills now and they'll last a lifetime and continue to bring you success. People respect someone who listens carefully. More importantly, those who listen are certain to catch important information that others don't.

Make the Effort

The first step to effective listening is to realize that listening takes effort. It won't happen on its own and it's not something that is going to take place automatically, just by your being there. Go into situations where it's important for you to listen. Be determined to listen, and listen carefully. Concentrate. It may be difficult at first, but in time you'll get better.

Pay Attention to the Speaker

It is difficult to listen to someone if you are not giving all your attention to that person. Ideally, you should look at the speaker's face the entire time she is talking. In a lecture, though, this is not always possible, because you also need to look up and down at your notes from time to time. Try, if you can, to write while keeping your eye on the professor. Your notes may look messier but, in time, you'll get more adept at writing without looking at the page. If you can't write and look at the professor at the same time, make certain to look up from your notes frequently. This will ensure that you are maintaining a direct line of communication with her.

If the professor is explaining a difficult concept, you are much better off not writing and simply looking her. This way, you can actively concentrate on listening and understanding. After the professor is finished, jot down a few notes or phrases to help you remember what was said.

Minimize Distractions

To maintain that direct line of communication between you and the speaker, it's important to minimize all outside distractions. Different things can be distracting. Perhaps there's someone very attractive who you always sit near in class and who occupies more of your attention than the professor. Maybe a friend you sit with can't resist chatting during the lecture. Even something as tame as chewing gum or a grumbling stomach can begin to sound like a major earthquake when you are trying to pay attention to something else. Select your seat carefully and come to class well-fed and prepared to listen.

Sit Properly

Additionally, the way you sit can also affect your ability to pay attention. If you slouch in the chair, your eyes won't be focused on the speaker. Each time you want to look at the teacher, you will have to lift up your entire head, and the effort needed to do that can disrupt your note-taking. Instead, it is much more effective to sit straight up with your back against the chair or seat back. Place the paper in the center of the desk or table and hold it in place with whichever hand you do not use to write. If you sit in this position, you should be able to watch the professor while writing; you also will be able to glance down at your notes by just moving your eyes, not your entire head.

Watch for Lapses

Become more attuned to the times when your mind is drifting to other subjects or your eyes are wandering out the window. When this happens, take a deep breath, open your mouth to breathe, and focus your attention back on the speaker immediately. Try stretching discreetly, or open your mouth to breathe instead of breathing through your nose. Or, sip some water from a water bottle to wake you up a little bit.

Be aware that everyone is prone to lapses in attention, and that if you can recognize when your mind wanders, you will begin to correct yourself much faster and not miss as much.

Work at It

Listening, like any skill, improves as you work at it. As you try to concentrate in different situations, you'll find you get better and better at it. Practice always helps.

Watch for Clues from the Speaker

Listening effectively means more than paying attention to the speaker's words. People convey a great deal of information through the way they speak as well as what they say. Get in the habit of concentrating on additional signals from a speaker besides spoken words. Pay attention to the speaker's tone of voice, the volume of their speech, pauses, hand gestures, and body language—these signals can enhance your understanding of the speaker's words. Additionally, by being alert to these elements in addition to spoken words, you have more to occupy your attention, ensuring that you remain actively engaged in the lecture, conversation, or discussion.

Participating in Class Discussions

When class participation is part of the grade, many students make the mistake of thinking that they just need to talk a lot to get a good grade. Beware, however, that there are many kinds of comments and questions, and some are much more intelligent and impressive than others.

Asking questions indicates your general interest in the class, but students who constantly raise their hands and ask very basic questions about fairly obvious points can make a bad impression—they appear too lazy to make an effort to understand something for themselves or think beyond the basic material to make connections to the real world or other subjects.

There is, however, a way to phrase a question that sounds more intelligent. For example, if you simply raise your hand and say, "I really don't get this. What does it all mean?" you sound like you just don't want to make the effort to understand the topic. On the other hand, if you say to a professor, "I see the point about Y and Z, but I'm having trouble understanding how they relate to X," you are asking a more specific question that reflects work to understand something. Try to make your questions as specific as possible to indicate you have some knowledge and a genuine interest in clarifying a point.

Another way students earn credit for class participation is by making comments during class discussions. Some students who feel compelled to say something in class will blurt out whatever pops into their heads. If the comment restates something that has already been said or merely points out something obvious, it won't impress the teacher; in fact, it can indicate you haven't been paying close attention. That is known as a "piggyback" answer, one that just hops onto something someone else says and does not demonstrate your original thought. If you want to make a general comment, make certain it contributes something meaningful or makes a new point.

Not everyone is comfortable participating in class discussions or asking questions in front of large groups. If you are one of those people, consider letting the teacher know outside of class that it is a challenge for you to speak out in class and participate verbally. Explain to the teacher why this is difficult for you, but also work on overcoming this fear or impediment since it is a lifeskill that will be important in future classes and in the workplace. Also, perhaps smaller class discussion sections will be a better place for you to have your voice heard. Look into taking a public speaking class, which might provide you with some confidence and tools to assist you in speaking in front of an audience. Not speaking up doesn't necessarily detract from the class participation portion of a grade. If you are shy or uncomfortable with offering comments in class, be sure to visit the professor during office hours and discuss the course—this will demonstrate that you have an active interest in the class.

QUOTE

"Whenever a bonus problem is listed on the board in math or a 'challenge word of the day' is listed for English, I *always* do the extra credit work. Math stumpers are usually hard but fun, and sometimes I bring them to my dad and we figure them out together when he gets home from work. I just treat extra credit like it is extra homework and try to earn more points since it protects me if I ever miss a homework assignment or bomb a test."

—Stacy B., Junior

CHAPTER 3

Class Selection

Think of choosing your classes like shopping for clothes. You can try things on for size, and then determine what is the best fit. Selecting your classes can be based on a variety of factors including teacher reputation, class reputation, your ability level in that discipline, and sometimes just what fits into your schedule. Read on to discover how to select classes that best suit your talents and interests.

Shopping for Classes

The first two weeks of any term, school year, or semester is affectionately known by many students as "the shopping period." With shiny new school supplies and sharpened pencils in hand, fresh-faced students venture out to class, ready to dive into new subject matter, explore new teachers and material, or continue with and explore more deeply the subject matter that they enjoy.

ESSENTIAL

Once you've narrowed down your options to just a few, collect the syllabi from each and plan to do the work the first two weeks in as many classes as you can juggle. It may be hectic or a bit overwhelming but in the end it will be worth it since you can explore your possibilities more deeply than you can by just skimming a course description.

Before you select classes, do some preliminary research. First and foremost, think about whether the subject matter is interesting to you. Read the course description and find out if there is a sample syllabus available to look at—ask at the department office or go online to look. Check out the reading list to see if it looks interesting. You can even go to the bookstore to look over the books themselves. To find out about a particular professor, ask around and talk to fellow students. Don't assume that just because a professor is famous or has won awards, he is a good teacher; schools sometimes hire big-name professors for their academic reputations, not for their teaching abilities. You might even try sitting in on a professor's class to see what he is like.

High School vs. College Shopping

In high school, a school college counselor or guidance counselor can help you find classes that are appropriate. If you're a freshman or sophomore in high school, you may not have much choice in the classes you can take. You're usually limited to choosing a class that is in either the regular college prep track, honors, or Advanced Placement (AP) level. Other than that, most courses in high school are simply basic requirements needing to be met. As you move into your junior and senior years, however, you may be able to choose some electives that match your interests. For example, you may get to pick which foreign language or science class to take to fulfill the graduation requirement.

ALERT

High school guidance counselors may know which courses are offered during each particular class period, so if you end up dropping a class, ask him or her to help you fill that time slot.

In college, on the other hand, you'll have more of a say in what you take, and scheduling is much more flexible since traditional courses are sometimes offered only twice per week or in the evenings. Some college students choose to stack all of their classes on Mondays, Wednesdays, and Fridays, for example. Once you do choose which classes you want, you may find yourself very eager to sign up for them! Some college students sleep out (literally, camp out!) to sign up for a popular class or go online the moment registration begins to seek enrollment in a course they want.

ESSENTIAL

Don't feel concerned about dropping a college class two weeks in; it doesn't mean you're a quitter. Remember, you're focusing on choosing a class that's the right fit for you.

Regardless of what grade you're in as you read this book, think of the first two weeks of any class as a time for you to gauge how a class will work for you. If the teacher is speaking at a pace that is way over your head or seems beyond the scope of what you have learned up to this point, chances are that class is not the right fit. If you're in high school, talk to your guidance counselor about how to tackle the class (perhaps by seeing a tutor to catch up), or change it if possible (to find a class at a level more suited to your background). If you're in college, consider dropping the class and finding another.

When to Choose Challenging Classes

Choose your classes wisely and carefully, both in high school and college. Straight As in honors and Advanced Placement classes mean something different than straight As in a regular college preparatory track with no advanced coursework. How can a college distinguish between its applicants from so many varied high schools? First understand this idea: colleges evaluate you by how you perform within the context of your school and what is offered there.

That's why you should consider signing up to take the hardest classes you are capable of surviving. Choose the most difficult classes you can take in the areas that come easiest to you and in which you more naturally excel. If you love history and have done well in prior history classes, an AP history class might be a good choice. But if you usually struggle at math, there's no sense in trying to tackle an advanced calculus class. A good rule of thumb is: If you think there is a chance you will get a C in the honors or AP class, take the regular level class. If you can pull an A or B, you should be stretching yourself to take honors or advanced level courses.

If you think it's a better idea to try to get straight As in regular track classes in order to "look good" for college, think again. Don't take the lazy or easy way out by just coasting through high school in regular track. Colleges will see right through that. Just do the best job you can and aim high by challenging yourself as much as you can. Why not?

In college, the same is true. Once you've narrowed down your field of study, go ahead and take the most challenging classes you can handle. Once you've graduated and are working, you'll be glad that you learned as much as you could in college. And, if you think you *may* plan to continue on and apply to graduate school, you want to show that you've challenged yourself in your coursework. Just like in high school, you want to show that you didn't take the easy way to a diploma.

Laziness and the Easy Way Out

Mark Twain once wrote, "Don't let school get in the way of your education." What he meant was that solely traditional classroom and book learning is not where all of your education takes place. There are a multitude of experiences beyond the four walls of your classroom that shape and educate you in different ways as well. Travel experiences, late-night talks in your dorm room, online learning, leadership and camp experiences, school clubs and organizations, and athletics are just a few other venues and experiences where you are educated.

QUESTION

What if I don't feel ready to attend college?
Students bloom at different times in their academic careers. For some, high school is a piece of cake and for others a painful struggle. Community college is a good alternative when you recognize you need to get yourself together and demonstrate to admissions that you have figured out how to be a better student.

Skipping class, sleeping late, relying on purchased lecture notes, or reading Cliff notes in lieu of doing your job of being a student always comes back to bite you in the form of bad grades or a bad reputation among your teachers and classmates. School is certainly full of temptations, distractions, and a multitude of activities to juggle simultaneously. If you opt to just coast through school by doing the bare minimum, you will not only be missing out on a great deal of learning and academic opportunities, but at some point your bad habits will come back to haunt you. And by the time this happens, it may be too late to dig yourself out of the hole you have created. Bad grades equal summer school, or community college as your only option after high school, or retaking a course, or Ds and Fs on your permanent transcript/academic record.

When to Take a Break

That being said, when schoolwork becomes such a chore that you find you're taking shortcuts and cheating yourself out of a deeper learning experience, then it may be time to take a personal pause from school. If you need a breather from school or some extra academic help or motivation, seek the guidance of your teacher, counselor, or even parents. Sometimes taking a break from school to re-focus or have a nontraditional educational experience, such as studying abroad or getting a job, is just the motivation you need to recharge your battery until you are ready to return and complete school. If you are thinking of this option, have a solid plan in place for what you'll do on your "break" (hint: it must be something constructive!) and how long it will last.

Class Selection and Transcript Analysis

Your transcript is a very important document that reflects all your courses and grades in school. College and graduate school admission officers will agree across the board that the number one factor in making admission or rejection decisions comes down to the transcript—the courses you take and the grades you earn as a student in your school. Yes, many other factors are considered when you apply to college or graduate school, including your standardized test scores, extracurricular involvement, jobs, volunteer experiences, summer experiences, internships, honors and awards, teacher recommendations, counselor report, personal statement, and other supplemental college essays. But, by and large, *the transcript demonstrates to admission officers your selections and achievements in those courses/academic disciplines and serves as the strongest indicator of the kind of student you are within the context of your own school.* Information about your academic performance is invaluable in predicting how successful you will be at the next level of your education.

Here is what colleges and graduate programs look for on a transcript and in your academic choices:

1. The degree of difficulty of the coursework you take within the context of your school.
2. Your grade patterns—a direct comparison between first and second semester, and year to year.
3. Trends shown by your grades: did your grades improve as you advanced each year or did they go down?
4. Whether you went beyond what was offered in your school: did you seek out additional academic experiences (such as community college, summer programs, independent study, or research)?

Let's look closer at each factor.

Degree of Difficulty

Colleges receive an academic profile from each high school listing all of the courses offered at every of the 40,000-plus high schools in America. This profile shows all of the classes available at the individual school including college prep courses, Advanced Placement (AP), or honors/accelerated classes. An admission officer evaluates each candidate not only based on the grades earned but the degree of difficulty of the course load the student followed.

Grade Patterns

Admission directors like to see students with grade patterns that improve or at minimum stay the same from one semester to the next. If you earned a B first semester, they look favorably if you earned a B+, or better yet, some form of an A second semester. (If the class is only a one-semester class than you should work even harder to do well, since there is only one shot to succeed.) That improvement demonstrates you have mastery of the subject or have grown to master the material over time as it gets more difficult or in depth.

On the other hand, a student whose grades tend to go down second semester sends a different message. Perhaps as the school year moves on and gets progressively more difficult, this student could not master the harder material. Or perhaps the student begins to "tune out" as the summertime approaches. That grade dip can imply either laziness as the school year goes on, lack of focus, or that the second semester was more academically challenging and you could not keep up. If all of your grades across the board drop in one particular semester that will send up red flags as well. Be prepared to justify the dip with an explanation to colleges (hopefully a legitimate one like you had mono or other long-term illness, experienced a loss or divorce in your family, etc.) as opposed to just saying "senioritis kicked in second semester!"

Grade Trends

Admission officers next address grade trends. How did a student do overall from freshman through junior year or high school or college? Did the grades make an upward turn throughout as the student matured or did things go in a downward trend over the course of each year? Again, the closer you get to higher level work (i.e., junior year and fall of senior year), the closer you are in the eyes of admission officers to being a potential student on their campus. The stakes keep getting higher the older you get and further along you are in school. Expectations increase about your ability, level of responsibility, and how actively you take learning and approaching courses into your own hands. If you're worried about your own grade trends, don't be afraid to seek help.

Additional Academic Experiences

For high school students: What if your school does not offer Advanced Placement (AP) or honors classes? Will you be penalized in the eyes of admission officers? Not if you explore other options. Here are some ideas of things you can do to supplement and enhance your transcript:

- Take an online class in a course that your school does not offer or in a more advanced level than your school offers. Please see Chapter 17 for information on how to find a reputable online course.
- Seek out courses at a local community college. Most of the time, courses are transferrable to your high school, and in some cases the grade you earn can even be added to your high school transcript.
- Approach a teacher in a class you enjoy(ed) and see if you could be a Teacher's Aide (T.A.) or if the teacher will do an independent study with you.

ALERT

Though you want to have fun your senior year, don't find yourself socializing and partying to the degree that it harms your grades and prevents you from having any college choices.

By all means, if you are not strong in math, then complete your high school's requirements and double up with an extra elective in a concentration that interests you more—start learning another language or artistic discipline, or add an extra class in an academic area that you enjoy and usually succeed in more. Bottom line: seek out and chart the path you want your school experience to be—even if that means thinking outside the box.

Save Your Old Papers

Clearly, course selection can impact your academic career later, so it's also useful to consider saving some of your old graded papers, writing, tests, research papers, or projects. Why? Here's one reason. Some programs will ask for a writing sample or example of good work you have done in high school or college. If you have saved some of your best work, complete with positive teacher comments, this request will be easy for you. Many students dump work at the end of the school year, only to realize later they may have been better off keeping some of it. Even a graded math test that shows your work and thought process can be insightful to admission officers. A paper you reprint off your computer is of less value than a graded one with teacher comments. So, save those papers with grades and teacher comments in case you are asked to provide photocopied samples later.

QUOTE

"I request a copy of my unofficial transcript each semester to be sure my grades are listed properly. I have actually found some mistakes along the way! I work hard to earn those grades, but they are ultimately input into a computer by a human being. People make mistakes so I want to be sure that I catch them!"

—Erica R., Senior

CHAPTER 4

Teachers Are People, Too

Your teachers are the bosses. But here is the thing: They also have lives outside of school, too. They don't just live at school to serve their students (although most are extremely passionate about what they do!). At the end of each day of work, teachers go home, do laundry, take showers, talk on the phone, watch TV, surf the Internet, exercise, and eat dinner. Whether it seems like it or not, teachers are people, too, and are ultimately there to educate, support, and help you. Don't forget: Teachers are doing their jobs but they do have a life outside of school. So it is very important, in fact *essential* if you want to succeed, that you show respect for your teachers and realize that they are people, too.

The Importance of Teacher Relationships

If you see your teacher outside of class in the hallway, parking lot, at the grocery store, wherever, what should you do? Look him in the eye, say hello, and show respect. The importance of teacher relationships can't be stressed enough. You want all your teachers (or at least the vast majority of them!) to view you as a "good kid." Even if you describe yourself as a shy person, step up to the plate and say hello. Better yet, when you see a teacher, try to think on your feet and make reference to something recent you did in class such as, "Hey, Ms. Smith. That was a brutal math test." Or, "Mr. Jones, have a great weekend. I'll be cranking out that paper!" Just say something—*anything*—that shows you are treating the adult who happens to be your boss with respect and friendliness.

Talking with your teachers is a great way to "practice" your interacting-with-adults skills. You will need them when you try to find a job, work with a community service coordinator, plan classes with your advisor or college counselor, or even interact with your religious leader such as a pastor or rabbi. Teachers are also great receptors for you to try to work out your academic (and sometimes even social) concerns. They will make useful suggestions to help you improve, and teachers appreciate students who come to them to seek help. Don't be afraid or intimidated, no matter what your classmates may say about a teacher. Teachers select this profession because they genuinely *want* to educate and connect with teens.

Here are some sample phrases to say to your teacher if you see him outside of class:

- Good: "Hey, Mr. Smith."
- Even better: "Hey, Mr. Smith, that bonus question was a toughie on the test today."
- Generic but fine: "Hi, Mr. Smith. Have a great weekend."
- Reference to current class work: "Mr. Smith, I'm working on my problem sets tonight!" (or some other reference to the work you are doing for his class)
- The million-dollar-quick-thinking-on-your-feet comment: "Mr. Smith, did you see the stock market numbers today on the news? It was just like what we talked about in class!" (This is a stellar way to make some connection to what you learned in class to the outside real world.

Teachers *love* this type of comment because it helps them know that you are really grasping what they're teaching.)

Are You a Kiss-up?

Chances are, some of your classmates will call you a kiss-up if you make an effort to talk to your teacher outside of class. The truth is, it's not kissing-up—it's being pleasant and respectful. And if your good relationship with your teacher helps you get a better grade, an exciting internship, or a great college recommendation letter . . . who gets the last laugh?

Take Pride in Your Work

Being a conscientious student means you take pride in your work; it indicates you are not just going through the motions of showing up for class, but are taking your work seriously. That, in turn, shows that you respect your teacher and the lessons that he or she is trying to teach you.

The quality of the work you turn in also indicates how conscientious you are. For example, an essay that has been carefully proofread and neatly printed shows you've put work into it and care about how it appears. An essay smudged with last night's dinner, your morning coffee, or pencil marks, and rife with spelling or grammatical errors sends the message that you really don't care that much about the work. That, in turn, says to your teacher/boss that you don't respect his class.

ESSENTIAL

Don't sweat the small stuff. You will make mistakes in school and will learn from them. Just don't let each small issue wear you down and don't worry that one goof will be emblazoned in your teacher's mind forever. While it may be a big deal to you, teachers have dozens, sometimes hundreds, of other students to also evaluate. Your one error will not stick out in their mind every time they see you.

While there are specific things to do that show how conscientious you are, you also need to adopt a committed attitude. Take pride in your work as a student, approach your job seriously, and everything you do will reflect this positive attitude. A committed attitude shows your teacher that you're willing to learn, and will help you transcend a poor quiz grade here and there.

Hold Yourself Accountable for Academic Mistakes

What happens if you bomb a test? Receive a poor grade you did not expect on an essay you wrote? Feel totally confused and frustrated in a particular class? Go to your teacher first. Be proactive and try to get help from your teacher before you involve your parents. Why? Because it is time for you to take charge of your academic experience. Don't be the student whose parents call the teacher every time you get a grade that disappoints you. And don't be the student whose teacher has to call his parents because he's not taking his work seriously.

If you don't feel comfortable approaching your teacher about the problem, then it's time to talk to your parents. They may be able to help you strategize what to say, or role-play you approaching your teacher.

ALERT

Of course, if you encounter any sort of harassment or inappropriate behavior on the part of your teacher, do not try to handle it yourself. Immediately involve your parents or a school authority.

Teachers respect students who stand up for themselves in a polite way, even if they don't agree with you. Be respectful and careful with your words, but do stand up for yourself when necessary. For example, if you disagree with an essay grade, ask the teacher nicely to help you understand why you got that grade. Ask what you could have done to earn a higher grade. Explain thoughtfully and specifically why you think your work was better than the grade indicates. Even if the grade doesn't change, you've showed the teacher that you care about your work.

Your Teacher Is Smarter Than You Think

Some students think they can easily outsmart the teacher. Keep in mind, though, that your teacher was once a student, too. Any tricks you think of, your teacher has probably thought of, too. Consider this popular story passed on from one student to another about an incident that supposedly took place at an American college. As the story goes, four college buddies decided to take a weekend ski trip, even though they had a major exam coming up that Monday afternoon.

They had a great weekend partying, but on their way home Monday morning, they realized none of them had studied. They decided to skip the exam and make up an excuse. When they went to class the following Wednesday, they told the professor they had been driving to class Monday morning from their off-campus apartment, when they'd gotten a flat tire several miles away from school. They tried to fix it as fast as they could, they said, but the flat detained them for several hours and forced them to miss the exam. The professor expressed sympathy for their plight and told them they could make up the exam that Friday. The four friends were thrilled that they got all this extra time to study.

They showed up at the classroom Friday completely prepared for the exam. The professor passed out the test and when the four friends turned over the exam, they were horrified to find this one question, "Which tire on your car had the flat?"

The moral of this story: Don't lie to your teacher. Respect the time he or she puts into preparing for the class, and be accountable for your behavior.

Finding a Mentor or Confidante

Your friends, family, and upperclassmen can offer you advice on many things, but a teacher is perhaps best qualified to offer specific advice about your education. For that reason, finding a faculty member who can serve as your mentor is extremely important. In addition to offering you advice, a mentor can help you negotiate the school's bureaucracy, discuss your future career or educational plans, write letters of recommendation, and much more.

Finding a mentor takes time and effort. There's no sign-up sheet for mentors, and no professor is going to knock on your door to volunteer. You need to find a teacher who you like and respect, and then work to establish a relationship. At some point, you will take a course with a teacher who you really like. You can initially see this person during office hours or after class. On the first couple of visits, simply discuss the course. If the professor seems receptive, you can eventually ask for advice on other aspects of your education and volunteer more information about your own interests and goals.

ESSENTIAL

Seek out a mentor who might be able to guide you further into an internship under their advisement or who can assist you in networking with colleagues or partners they know in the working world. Mentors do not have to be teachers. They can also be coaches, employers, school administrators, graduate students, or residential advisors.

If you meet with the teacher or professor several times during the semester, you should begin to feel you are establishing a relationship. The key to finding a professor who becomes your mentor, though, is to maintain that relationship once the class is over. Don't let a solid relationship with a teacher slip away. Make certain you continue meeting with the teacher, even if you are no longer taking her class. This won't be too difficult to do if he or she has become involved in helping you plan your future in some way.

If you do not find a teacher mentor from a course you have taken, other adult figures also serve as excellent mentors. Coaches, spiritual leaders (your priest or rabbi), or teachers who serve as liaisons to clubs or organizations in which you participate may mentor you. An extra adult sounding board outside of your own parents is always a helpful addition to the support network you build for yourself.

Making a Good Impression

There's no way around the fact that grades are a central part of measuring success at most schools. A large portion of a grade is based on objective information, such as the number of short-answer questions you got right or wrong or the number of days you attended class. A small part of your grade, however, is subjective: It is based in large part on the teacher's impression of you. While this impression can't change the number of exam responses you got right or wrong, it can influence other aspects of your final grade. For example, a final grade will often reflect a grade for class participation or effort, which is much more difficult to quantify than the number of right or wrong responses.

It is extremely important that you try to make a good impression. You also need to be careful how you do it. If you overdo your effort, it can seem insincere and backfire. For example, if you interrupt the lecture or class discussion simply to make some comment that you think demonstrates how smart you are, you will not impress the teacher. Moreover, the teacher might resent that you've interrupted class for an unrelated point in an obvious attempt to gain Brownie points.

The impression you want to convey is not necessarily how smart you are, but that you are a conscientious student who is willing to work hard to learn. There are a couple of specific things you can do to make this impression: Have a great attendance record, and visit the teacher outside of class.

Have a Perfect Attendance Record

Nothing is more off-putting to a teacher than a student who consistently arrives late to class, or doesn't attend at all. Coming late disrupts the entire class and, more severely, indicates to the teacher that you don't care about the class. Even in a large lecture course, where you think you might slip in unnoticed, a teacher can spot you coming in late. You should, therefore, make it a habit to get to class on time. If you have a special reason for being late, make certain you see the professor during office hours to explain the situation and apologize. Even better, tell the professor ahead of time if possible so she has a heads-up.

Don't attend class ill with a fever, visibly sick, or contagious. While you want to try to have a perfect attendance record, your teachers and classmates do not want to be exposed to your germs or illness. No one enjoys being sneezed or coughed upon in class.

Coming late to class is a disruption; not coming at all is a major problem that can seriously affect your grade. In some smaller classes, a teacher will take attendance. If this is the case, you should obviously make certain you go as often as possible. Having perfect attendance will probably impress the teacher when it comes time to make your class participation grade.

Even if a teacher does not take attendance, it is still worth going to class as often as you can. For one thing, being there on a regular basis ensures that you are exposed to all the course material, which in itself will probably improve your grade. Moreover, if you attend class regularly, the teacher will recognize you as a familiar face.

Make the Most of Office Visits

If a teacher doesn't know you by name, however, it won't matter what image she has of you when she gives you a grade. While a teacher will usually know you by name in a small class or seminar, it is almost impossible for her to know you personally in a large lecture class. You should, therefore, make certain to see the professor at least once during office hours to introduce yourself.

There are many reasons why teachers hold office hours. First, teachers want to offer a time to be accessible outside of class to their students to foster a more personal dialogue and provide attention to students who seek it. Also, office hours provide students opportunities to discuss problems, concerns, or questions they have with the subject matter or grades they may have received that concern them.

When you do visit your teacher's office, be prepared with your questions and comments so that they do not feel you are wasting their time. To help break the ice, try to come up with a specific question to ask about the class or about a particular lecture. During the course of your discussion, you can tell the professor a bit about yourself and your academic interests and aspirations. Doing this ensures that the teacher has an impression of you as an individual, not as another face in the crowd. Here are some suggestions of what to say or do when you see them for office hours:

- Review essays you have written and seek additional guidance based on their comments;

- Bring in tests or quizzes with answers you got wrong and ask to review them;
- Prepare a comment you have considered or debate a point they made (as long as you substantiate it) to demonstrate that you have thought about what you learned in class and applied it to the world outside of class;
- Bring in any other questions from class notes, handouts, or readings that may have confused you.

Don't be shy about visiting your teachers outside of class time and building an independent rapport with them.

Teacher Recommendations

Those teacher relationships will pay off tenfold when it comes time to ask for a recommendation for a summer program, college, graduate program, or job. Teacher recommendations are testimonies that educators provide your colleges, graduate schools, or future employers about your performance and contributions in their classes. The comments in these recommendations are taken very seriously and serve as an important piece of selection criteria. Sometimes they are the only way an evaluator can get a real sense of who you are as a classmate or team player, which offers them an indication of your potential as a college or graduate student or future employee. The better a teacher knows you and the more support and advance notice they have in writing your recommendations, the better.

Here are some ideas on how to obtain terrific, personal teacher recommendations:

- Build good relationships with your teachers by sitting close to the front in their classes, doing extra credit assignments, frequenting office hours, being friendly whenever you see them outside of class, and so on.
- When you ask your teacher to write you a recommendation, provide him with a copy of your student resume or "brag sheet," which lists your extracurricular activities, community service, awards, honors, jobs, hobbies, and interests. (More on this to come.)

- Ask your teacher(s) to write *well* in advance of the deadline.
- Provide your teacher with a sample of graded work from her class with comments, if applicable.
- Jot down some bullet points of ways you have contributed to her class (this is sometimes called a "student blurb").
- Write a thank-you note and let the teacher know where you were admitted and how their letter helped, when applicable.

There are a few items to give to your teacher when they agree to write recommendations for you. A brag sheet is important to share with your teacher. In addition to the brag sheet, you will need a student blurb.

Build Your Brag Sheet

A brag sheet is a place for you to list everything you have done outside of your classroom—after school, on the weekends, and during summers. It is basically an extracurricular resume. List all honors, awards, accomplishments, extracurricular activities, summer experiences, internships, employment, community service, and athletics in which you have participated or achieved, as well as hobbies and interests that you have. Include a column listing the hours per week and weeks per year dedicated to each activity. Keep this growing log in a document on your computer and track your involvement since the summer after eighth grade. Don't forget about any awards or honors you have won in these activities!

Following is a sample brag sheet. If you begin your log the summer after eighth grade, by senior year you will be ready to list your activities on college applications.

LAST NAME, FIRST NAME, MIDDLE INITIAL (SOCIAL SECURITY NUMBER OR DATE OF BIRTH)

Activity	School Years	Hours per week/ Weeks per year	Positions/Honors/Descriptions
Sports & Athletic Awards/Honors			
Name of School Varsity Track	9–12	25 / 26	Varsity (9–12), Most Valuable Distance Runner (11), League Champions (11), finished 5th in the 800 M at CIF SS Division III Finals (11), League Champions and CIF SS Division III Champions (10), finished 9th in the 800 M at CIF SS Division III finals (10)
Name of School Varsity Cross Country	11, 12	25 / 26	Varsity (11, 12), League Champions and CIF SS Division III Champions (11), 5th place team at State Championships (4th place runner on the team) (11)
Name of School Junior Varsity Volleyball	9, 10	30 / 26	League Champions (9, 10), Setter position
Orange County Volleyball Club	9	18 / 48	Setter position, Attended Volleyball Festival in Reno, Nevada
Newport Hills Swim Team	9–11	10 / 30	Qualified for and swam in the League Final Championship Meet and Relay Finals all three seasons
Community Service			
Assistance League "Assisteens"	9–12	3 / 50	Treasurer (12), Recording Secretary (11), Chairman (10), Assistant Chairman (9), Aiding community through service projects: Community Thrift Shop, Operation School Bell, Kids on the Block, Someone Cares Soup Kitchen, Oasis Senior Center Pancake Breakfast, worked with children at Interfaith Shelter and Girl's Inc. on events such as: Valentine's Day Party and Halloween Party, made blankets, Easter baskets, Christmas stockings, personal care kits, teddy bears, donated clothing, and participated in various other projects
Interfaith Shelter	12	2 / 48	Help plan and organize a birthday party for the children monthly; in charge of arts and crafts
LIFT	12	5 day program	Learn leadership skills from successful people in the community
Organizations & Clubs			
National Honor Society	10–12	2 / 40	Honored for academic and extracurricular achievements, organize community service projects, weekly meetings, and ongoing community service projects
French Club	9, 10	2 / 40	Learn about culture and practice speaking

continued

Activity	School Years	Hours per week/ Weeks per year	Positions/Honors/Descriptions
Academic Awards & Honors			
Academic Letter with Honors	11		Above 4.0 GPA
Academic Honor Roll	9–11		Above 4.0 GPA every semester
Employment / Summer Experiences			
Zinc Cafe	11, 12	20 / 12	Greet customers, take orders, use cash register, deliver food to tables
Newport Hills Swim Team Coach	9, 10	8 / 12	Coached youngsters in group swimming; paid job
Cal Coast Track Club Summer Running Program	9–12	18 / 12	Beach run every morning at 6:30 a.m. and speed workouts two times per week at night
Cal Coast Track Club Mammoth Camp	9–12	5-day overnight camp in August	Ran trails in the high altitude and live with the team; plan and participate in skits and talent show activities
UCSB Volleyball Summer Camp	10	4-day overnight camp	Lived on campus and attended volleyball skills camp with college coaches and players
Stanford Volleyball Summer Camp	10	4-day overnight camp	Lived on campus and attended volleyball skills camp with college coaches and players
UCLA Volleyball Summer Camp	9	4-day overnight camp	Lived on campus and attended volleyball skills camp with college coaches and players
Hobbies and Interests: scuba diving, snorkeling, cooking, snowboarding, pets, and sailing			

When writing a brag sheet or any resume, list your jobs or history in reverse chronological order, meaning, the most recent to the furthest back in time. Also, list items in terms of most hours committed to least hours committed to an activity to demonstrate what activity required more of your time.

Write a Student Blurb

A student blurb is a short, bulleted list of your individual accomplishments and reflections on your contribution in a particular class. In it, you can list some highlights of your recollections of the course along with any real examples of how you added to the classroom experience through a particular debate, conversation, or question. The more specific examples you can recall about your performance in the class, the better.

You will give your student blurb to your teacher along with your brag sheet (just discussed) so he or she can use the information to help formulate a recommendation. If you are lucky, your teacher may sprinkle in some of the actual tidbits you wrote about yourself into the recommendation as if they were her own comments. Teachers have dozens of these to write a year and they are time-consuming; the more assistance, support, and lead time you can give to them to aid in the process, the better. Here is a sample student blurb:

Honors World History Class
Cindy Muchnick, Class of 2014
Junior Year, Teacher: Mr. Jones

1st Semester Grade: A
2nd Semester Grade: A-

Highlights of the course for me:
I enjoyed applying history to my real life when we studied inventions and I wrote my project on the contact lens as a miraculous invention (see attached).

I participated greatly in a heated discussion about the Industrial Revolution, siding with the big business owners.

I enjoyed the field trip to the colonial museum and asked many questions regarding how foods were made back then.

I was challenged by the speed and pace of the class but it helped me to visit you during office hours weekly.

I thought learning about art history during the Renaissance was incredible to see the interdisciplinary way I can learn. Did my artist paper on Leonardo da Vinci and received an A.

I worked independently on my own to research World War II airplanes for extra credit assignment.

Write a Thank-You Note

Always thank a teacher for taking time to write you a recommendation. Teachers are not paid any extra money to spend time writing thoughtfully about you. A proper thank-you note and even gift card as a gesture is always appreciated and is good etiquette and practice. Make sure your thank you is not e-mailed or left in a voicemail but handwritten, the old-fashioned way. Below is a simple example you can follow and modify for your purposes.

Dear Mr. Jones,

Thank you again for taking the time out of your busy schedule to write me a recommendation letter. I realize this is extra work for you and wanted to thank you for your willingness to write on my behalf. I have enjoyed being your student. **[Plus add one personal sentence about you/the teacher.]**

Thanks again,
Cindy Muchnick

QUOTE

"My science teacher is a real toughie. Everyone warned me I got into the 'wrong' science class. Bummer for me. Actually, I realized that Mr. Jasper has a soft spot for kids who talk a lot in class. He likes participation. So I am sure to have my comments or questions ready and know that if I contribute a lot I will be on his good side! Plus, I heard he doesn't like it when parents call or get involved if kids get bad grades. I made my mom promise not to e-mail or call him without asking me first so I could decide if it was something I could handle on my own."

—Steven T., Junior

CHAPTER 5

Time Management

While "management" seems to be a term often used for those with careers and adults in the business world, remember that you have a job, too: being a student. To do this job well, you need to gain some of your very own managerial skills. When it comes to allocating and breaking down your time into useful, practical, worthwhile chunks for studying, class time, socializing, extracurricular activities, sleep, exercise, meals, and more, you are the manager of your time. Time is precious and time does fly, so divide it up accordingly, and spend and use it wisely.

Basic Time Management Strategies

There are twenty-four hours in a day, approximately eight of which you use to sleep, eight of which you attend your school or job, and the other eight are filled with every other task in your life including homework, extracurricular activities, socializing, family obligations, work, eating, doing laundry, going to the gym, grocery store, etc. How you choose to spend your time can make or break your academic career.

ALERT

Wear a watch or carry a device that easily tells you the time. Set your watch five minutes fast. It can help keep you on time.

Managing your time takes a plan or a heightened awareness of what tasks need to be accomplished in a certain amount of time. Meeting deadlines in an organized manner allows you to enjoy not only the result of your efforts, but also the journey and hard work it takes to achieve results.

Here are a few time management exercises you can try:

- Count how many hours you spend on the main activities in your life: school, transportation, work, athletics, extracurricular activities, socializing, eating, sleeping, studying, etc. and compare your list against the 168 hours there are in a week. This will give you an idea of how much of a handle you have on your time. This exercise can be a real wake-up call if you never seem to know how you ran out of time to get everything done.
- Don't spend more time anticipating and worrying than acting. Instead, take active steps in planning out your time and begin to take action. The famous quote by Nike, "Just do it," has become a significant statement in our culture and celebrated for a reason.
- Try to spend time organizing e-mails and electronic files into a filing system and delete what you don't need. Just as you throw away junk mail you receive through snail mail, don't be afraid to delete items in your inbox. File away content that you may need access to later in an orderly manner. The same goes for paper files. Dump what you don't

need and organize in a filing system what you do need. Taking the extra moment to follow an organization system will save you hours of frustration and searching later.

- Pencil in a schedule by half-hour blocks for times when you are scheduled for something (class, appointment, workout, practice, etc.) and you can literally see where you have holes or gaps of time to fill with more or even a pause.

Also, remember there is often "dead time" built into your school day. Sometimes free periods or a break between classes can serve as "found time." Instead of socializing or procrastinating, use those free periods as a time to get ahead on your work.

Create a To-Do List

Whether you jot your list on a piece of scrap paper or keep it on your cell phone, maintain a running list of things to do. Though you may think that you are able to remember and recall everything without writing it down, something will slip through the cracks. Write down your list!

Another benefit to writing down your list is that you can cross off or delete items from it. You can enjoy a sense of accomplishment in completing a task, no matter how mundane, and it means one less thing to worry about. Quickly, however, that crossed-off item will likely be replaced by something else. Think of your to-do list as though it is an endless load of laundry. Once you catch up washing and folding, there are always more dirty clothes close behind!

Keep your list with you at all times for reference. If you are extra organized, consider prioritizing your list in order of importance or grouping tasks into categories based on where you need to do or accomplish them (i.e., things located geographically nearby one another) or by theme such as: homework, sports, personal.

Effective Scheduling

Many study guides instruct you to set a rigid schedule for yourself in which each minute of each day is devoted to fulfilling a certain task. These schedules block off time for everything from study sessions to mealtimes to hours when you can sleep. But here's the problem: Schedules like these are virtually impossible to always follow. What if, for example, you don't feel like eating dinner at exactly 6:30 on a particular night? What if you are supposed to study from 8:00 to 11:00 on Tuesdays, but one week your professor wants you to attend a guest lecture at the same time? What if there is a really good party on a Friday night you want to go to, but you don't have time scheduled for it? What do you do?

Look at the Big Picture

Student life is far too chaotic to be squeezed into a neat, orderly schedule. Your schedule will change frequently: One week you may have a major exam or a paper due, which will require more work, while another week, you may have to devote substantial time to an extracurricular activity. Even weekly study tasks, such as reading lecture notes or assigned texts, will take different amounts of time. One week the assigned readings may be very difficult and take twelve hours to complete, while another they'll be substantially easier and only take four hours. But if you are stuck in a rigid schedule, you won't be able to make the necessary adjustments to provide the time you need.

ALERT

Invest in a small egg timer, which you can purchase at your local grocery store. If you need to be reminded of your increments of studying or your schedule, a timer's bell will alert you. Old-fashioned timers are easier than programming cell phones or PDA devices to keep you in check.

You do, however, need to have *some* kind of schedule so that you can keep track of what needs to be done and leave yourself enough time to do it. Instead of making a rigid schedule, you can plan a more general one that will allow you to make changes on a week-to-week and day-to-day basis. This general schedule only shows those activities you do every week of the semester at the exact same times. You should make it up at the beginning of the semester, before classes have actually started. Make a chart listing days of the week at the top, and the hours of the day in a column on the left side. Or, you can choose to make your schedule through a computerized program such as iCal or Yahoo Calendar, but be sure you have a portable version with you accessible though your PDA, Blackberry, iPad, or printouts of a few weeks at a time that you can carry around in your backpack, to adjust, write on, and refer to as necessary.

First, find out the meeting times of all your classes, and block off those times on the schedule. Then mark off any times you will be consistently unavailable to study; for example, those times when you are part of a club or a team. As shifts occur in scheduling, such as an added review session before final exams or a study group emerges, be sure to promptly note them in your calendar as well.

After you've blocked off those hours, you'll be able to see the times each day that are "free." Those "free" times can be spent any number of ways—studying, doing work, socializing with friends, etc. You can decide each week exactly how you can best utilize those "free" times.

▼ **SAMPLE WEEKLY LIST OF TASKS AND TIMES**

Read Articles for Psych	Sun., Tues. Evenings (2 hrs.)
Read Chapters 1–5 of Huck Finn	Mon. Evening (1–2 hrs.)
Read Chapters 5–10 of Huck Finn	Wed. Evening (1–2 hrs.)
Study for Bio Quiz on Thursday	Tues., Wed. Night
Meet with Group to work on project for Soc.	Sun. Afternoon (4 hrs.)
Read Chapter 14 for Sociology	Tues. Evening (1 hr.)
Finish Poem for Lit. Magazine	Mon.–Wed. Night (after 11 P.M.)
Go over Notes from Lectures, Readings	Sat. (4 hrs.)
Library Research for Soc. project	Mon.–Thurs. Midday (between classes)

During the week, work on each specific task during the time you've designated. Don't force yourself to spend an exact amount of time on each one since these are guesstimates of how much time a task will take you. Take each task as it comes; some will take more time than you anticipate, some will take less. Just make certain that by the end of the week you've fulfilled all the tasks you set for yourself.

In addition to making a weekly list of specific tasks, it's a good idea to make one for each day. Before you go to sleep each night, you can quickly make a list of the things you need to do the following day. You can include, in addition to study tasks, any specific errands you need to run, from doing laundry to returning books to the library. That way, you've got all your tasks in one place and you won't forget to do something. As you do each one, cross it off the list so you can see yourself making progress and feel you are accomplishing something.

Prioritizing Your Schedule

Some weeks, you will have an especially heavy workload and face a severe crunch for time. To prioritize your tasks, look at your list for the week and try to put them in order of importance. For example, completing an assignment that must be handed in or studying for a major exam are going to take priority over most other activities. Prioritize what is not only due at your first deadline but also what may take you the longest to finish or the assignment or task that you find the most difficult. Expend your energy when you are the freshest (i.e., at the outset of your task, early morning, and so on) on work that is more challenging for you and harder to accomplish.

After identifying what is most important for that week, make certain you devote most of your time to fulfilling those tasks. If you finish them, spend the remaining time on the less important ones. If you don't get to the less important tasks, you can make up for it in later weeks when your workload is less heavy. Just be certain you catch up at some point so you don't fall too far behind.

Finding Time for Everything Else!

Of course, everyone needs time away from work, but you shouldn't "schedule" in these times. As a student, your priority is fulfilling your study requirements, as well as commitments to extracurricular activities. These will take up a certain portion of time each week. When they are completed, any time that remains is yours to do with as you please.

ESSENTIAL

Always factor in plenty of time for sleep! Be sure your schedule does not get too full to limit that essential task of getting some zzz's.

Study Schedules for Exams

In general, you should avoid studying too far before an exam because you want the material you've prepared to remain fresh in your mind. At the same time, you need enough time to go over your notes, read your textbooks, and perhaps get extra help. To provide enough time to accomplish all this, you should begin studying about *five to seven days* before the examination.

Divvying Up Study Time

Try to divide your study preparation into several stages. The first stage, which you should do in one sitting, is to read through all your notes and create the master lists, which we'll discuss in Chapter 10. Make certain you designate a large block of time (probably about four to six hours for each course) at the beginning of your study preparation period for this purpose.

ESSENTIAL

Don't write down real deadlines on your calendars; always move them earlier by a few days. If your paper is due the eighth, then write that it is due the fifth. This will help ensure your work is done on time and "trick" you into thinking it is due sooner. (Kind of like setting your watch five minutes earlier than the actual time to be sure you arrive on time!)

The second bulk of your study preparation should be devoted to working with your study materials. Finally, if you have the time, you can also read additional sources.

Please see Chapters 10 and 11 for more detailed information about studying for exams.

Using Free Periods

It is called a free period since technically it is a block of time off that you have free to do what you please. Don't let the word "free" fool you, though. Even though you are "given" this time to do what you want, in school you need to think about maximizing all your free or found time to address your weakest academic areas. Can you use a free period to do some extra studying and review for an upcoming test? Or maybe you can use it to attend office hours for a teacher you never are free to meet due to scheduling conflicts? Can you encourage classmates to share study tips, notes, and quiz one another during your common free periods? Absolutely.

ALERT

Sometimes a class gets cancelled at the last minute because there is no substitute teacher prepared to teach the missed lesson. Bingo! You have just received the gift of free time to use at your discretion.

Set Goals for Yourself

As you get bogged down in the day-to-day life of being a student, you may find yourself spending time daydreaming about what you'll do when you're done with school. Instead of letting those daydreams rob you of free time, channel that energy into reminding yourself why you're working so hard in the first place.

Big-Picture Goals

To determine a big-picture goal, consider your purpose in attending school in the first place. If the only reason is because your parents or the government said you must, you are not going to be very happy. There must be *something* you hope to gain in your studies, and it doesn't necessarily have to be the same thing your parents or teachers want or expect. You may, for example, want to develop specific skills to help you in a certain career. Or, you might want to receive high grades so you can get into the graduate school of your choice. There might be more personal factors involved as well, such as the desire to better yourself, to become a more educated person, and to experience new ways of thinking and seeing.

Your "big picture" is a personal one, and it can be different from everyone else's. Keep this big picture in mind as you study and navigate school. Without a sense of this big picture, you can easily feel unfocused; however, if you maintain a clear sense of what you are doing and why, you are more likely to remain on track.

Try to see how each task you go about in your to-do lists and schedule fits into your big-picture goal. If you see how each agenda item contributes something to your goals, you'll remain much more focused on your work; you'll also find your studies more fulfilling.

Smaller Goals

Goals don't have to be simply big-picture, though. For each to-do list item, you should set a short-term goal, such as reading a chapter of a textbook thoroughly or studying for an upcoming exam. At the same time, though, you should set larger goals for your entire education and understand that all of the short-term goals help you get closer to the big one.

Avoiding Extracurricular Overload

If you find that your after-school activities are taking up too much of your time, find an excuse to limit just one of those activities by one practice, rehearsal, or meeting.

If you are an athlete with a large time commitment of multiple practices per week, consider telling your coach that your parents (or if you are in college just tell them you need extra help) are now requiring you to work with a tutor weekly to improve your grades. This request will not make the coach happy but will "buy" you two to three more hours of free time per week by giving up just one practice per week. If you tell a coach that you will need to miss one practice per week for academic reasons (until your grades improve), you will likely still be able to play in games. It's important to remember that although extracurricular activities are a great addition to your academic life, they are just that—an "extra." Your main job is to be a good student. Just be honest and offer yourself the best opportunity for success. Found time can relieve so much pressure and sometimes you need to find it by eliminating something from an already overbooked calendar.

If a large chunk of your extracurricular time is spent doing any activity other than a sport, such as a school club, theater, musical instrument, etc. you can also use this same request. Tell the leader that you need to miss one of the weekly commitments in order to get some tutoring to improve your grades. Simply limiting one major activity like this for one day will help you recover some "lost" time.

Conversely, do not drop an activity that meets only once weekly unless you feel it is not one you enjoy or want to continue. Missing an activity that meets just once can put you way behind, versus cutting out one meeting of a repetitive activity.

Avoiding Procrastination

"I'll save it for later," "I'll get to it . . . eventually," "Maybe next time?" These excuses mean that you are suffering symptoms of procrastination. Who wants to do schoolwork or study for a test or write a paper when the sun is shining and the beach or park is beckoning, or the newest Xbox game was just released and you just have to try it out? Or maybe the newest block-buster film has just been released.

What Makes You Procrastinate?

Temptations are all around you, such as:

- Your computer, often the very tool you need to access or complete a work assignment, is loaded with games, distracting music, and, of course, the Internet!
- Your friends who text, call, IM, Skype, or visit and want to hang out and not study.
- Your TV, iPod, iTouch, cell phone, or other electronic gadget that is much more fun to interact with than a boring homework assignment or vocabulary flashcards.
- Restaurants, the refrigerator, coffee shops, shopping malls, your car, etc.

You're not going to want to study every time you are supposed to. Nevertheless, you're going to have to motivate yourself somehow to do work even when you don't feel like it.

Using a Reward System

Avoid procrastination by setting up a system of rewards as motivation. For example, give yourself any time left after you've completed your study tasks for a particular day as your personal free time. This in itself serves as a reward to get you motivated to work. For example, if you know you want to watch television at night, you can force yourself to work efficiently during the day. Similarly, if you want to go skiing one weekend, you'll try your hardest to get all your work done during the week. You just need to remind yourself of the fun activities waiting for you when you are finished working.

Even with the promise of free time as a reward, you may still find it difficult to get motivated and begin working. If that's the case, provide yourself with additional rewards as you study. Set small goals, and reward yourself each time you fulfill them. For example, if you have several hours blocked off on Tuesday night for reading forty pages, promise yourself a snack after you've gotten halfway through the assignment. This will at least get you started. Work in smaller increments, such as twenty minutes at a time, and then stretch, drink a beverage, eat an m&m, or respond to an e-mail. Then, go back to work for another twenty minutes and so on until the increments can become longer and more bearable (which often depends on the subject or type of work you are doing).

These rewards don't need to be extravagant. A reward can simply be a short break to do something you like—getting ice cream, talking on the phone, going for a walk, listening to music, whatever. Just make certain the "reward" time is a short break lasting no more than twenty to thirty minutes.

This reward system is particularly helpful if you have to spend long hours at work, such as studying for an exam or writing a paper. If you think of how you'll be slaving away for many long hours, it will be extremely difficult to motivate yourself to begin. If you divide the task into several smaller ones, however, and promise yourself a small reward at the completion of each one, it will be much easier to get started. You know then that when you sit down to work, a reward of some kind is not all that far away.

When you finish a major task, such as completing an essay or taking a final exam, it's nice to give yourself a bigger reward—download some new songs or have a fun night out. These rewards will help you get through the especially difficult work periods during the school year.

QUOTE

"It used to feel overwhelming as a college student, like my time was not my own; the clock was always ticking, and classes and homework dictated my life. That anxious feeling I had all changed now that I have an effective organization system in place. Now *I* am in control of what I do when. Now time blocks are pre-planned and what I do during that time is pre-scheduled and blocked out, giving me a better sense of control."

—Marcie L., Sophomore

CHAPTER 6

Taking Notes in Class

While it is important to be a good listener and participant in class, you also need to master the art of taking good notes so that later you can refer back to them. Note-taking is a process that some find tedious, while others find to be barely an effort. Finding a system that works for you is an important task that will make the rest of your student life easier. As your workload becomes greater and the content of what you learn more sophisticated, so must your notes reflect that growth in your learning.

Why Bother Taking Notes?

So much of what you learn, retain, and will be tested on in school comes from attending class and becoming a competent note-taker. Many teachers and professors offer information in their lectures that goes above and beyond what's in your textbook or other class materials. And that additional information inevitably ends up on an exam!

The good news is, if you approach note-taking as a job, or a skill you can master, you will build a solid foundation that will help you achieve academic success. Once you have mastered the art of being an active listener in class (see Chapter 2), you will notice your note-taking skills improve greatly.

Here's a seven-step outline of an effective strategy for taking notes in class:

1. Arrive on time
2. Make preparations
3. Write down all key terms
4. Develop your own shorthand
5. Include brief definitions and explanations of key terms (wherever possible)
6. Construct a rough outline
7. Note general themes of the lecture

The better and more committed you are to devising a strong in-class system of note-taking, the better off you will be later when you need to use your notes to review or complete assignments out of class.

Step #1: Arrive on Time

That's right, the first step is pretty easy! Even better than arriving on time: Arriving a few minutes early if you can. It's difficult to take effective notes on the first few minutes of the lecture if you rush to class, arriving out of breath and flustered. By coming early, you can relax and decompress for a few minutes and put yourself in the right frame of mind. If you have time, you should review your notes from the previous class to help focus your attention on the day's subject matter.

Besides helping you get settled, arriving on time is just common courtesy. Dashing in late can distract and offend the teacher, and it's never a good idea to upset the professor.

Step #2: Make Preparations

When you get to class, take out a new sheet of paper or flip to a new page in your notebook. You should always start each class with a fresh piece of paper because lectures tend to have their own separate topics or themes. By keeping separate notes, you can better identify distinct themes.

ESSENTIAL

Have the right writing instrument to take great notes: Select a decent ballpoint for taking notes in class and have an extra available.

Always put the date and subject at the top of the first sheet, so you can put them in the proper binder or file at home. While spiral-bound notebooks may seem the easiest, most efficient, and lightest weight option for your bookbag, consider instead using plain, single-sheet looseleaf paper and binders instead. One thin binder for each class will allow you to move pages of notes around as you add to or modify what you do in class. It also allows you to insert handouts you received from your teacher next to your notes about that particular subject.

Next, consider drawing a line down the page about three inches from the left edge of the paper, so that you have an extra-wide margin (most pieces of notebook paper already have about a one and a half inch margin) to allow you more space to divide your notes to the right and left of a page. (More on that next.)

During class, take notes only on the right side of the margin. Leave the left side totally blank—you'll be using that space when you get to stage two, working on notes outside of class. You should also take notes on only one side of the paper; you'll use the backside later.

Make certain you have plenty of paper on hand throughout the lecture. Always put the date and subject on the top of each sheet; that way, if sheets from different days and classes get mixed up, you'll be able to figure out their proper sequence. And for each new sheet, continue drawing that line and taking notes only on the right side.

Have the right tools to take great notes. Loose-leaf paper (that's the kind with three holes that you can put in and take out of a binder notebook) works best so you won't have to bring your entire binder to class. It also enables you to add additional notes, rewrite notes, or shift pages without difficulty, and to file them away easily after the semester is over. Always put a date on each page!

Step #3: Write Down All Key Terms

The first and foremost commandment of note-taking is this: You cannot write down everything the professor says. This is so important that it bears repeating: *You are not going to be able to write down everything the professor says! Nor should you!* If you try to write down everything the professor says, you'll find yourself in deep trouble. At some point, no matter how fast you can write, you will miss something. Either you won't hear clearly, or you'll become distracted, or your hand will cramp up. And then, if you're like many students, you'll panic. As you struggle to figure out what you missed, you'll miss even more. And before you know it, you won't have notes for the majority of the lecture.

So let's make it clear right from the beginning. *You don't have to write down everything.* Your next question probably is, "So what exactly am I supposed to write down?" In order to answer that question, we need to examine the purpose of taking notes.

In taking notes, your aim should *not* be to create an exact transcript of the professor's lecture. If that were the case, the professor would simply hand out photocopies. A great deal of what you hear in class might be familiar to you and, therefore, doesn't really need to be recorded. Writing down information and concepts that are new and unfamiliar should be your priority.

Identify the Key Terms

During lectures, the main thing professors do is to communicate new information. The majority of it is specific, such as names of people or places, significant dates, certain theories, formulas, and concepts. These are the *key terms* of the lecture.

Most often, these terms are going to be new to you, making them harder to remember. A goal of note-taking, then, is to keep track of all these key terms. Your professor may even write down key terms on the board or spell them out for the class. That's a great indicator that you should take note of this concept. You should *always* note anything a teacher writes on the board. But there will also be many other terms that a professor might not write—if these are new to you, make certain you write them down as well.

ALERT

Pencils may seem like a good idea for note-taking because you can erase and edit with them; but they break and wear down, leaving you to sharpen (or click or twist them) and deal with eraser shavings in class. Pencil is also harder on your eyes to read than ink due to the paper glare.

Believe it or not, if you write down just these key terms, you'll have a pretty accurate representation of the entire lecture. These terms are most often the highlights and key points around which the entire lecture is based. You can be certain that if you showed your professor this list of terms, she would be able to recreate the lecture for you in its entirety. Can you?

You might be surprised how much you actually remember merely by noting key terms. As long as you've been listening carefully, these terms can serve as triggers that help you recall much of what you heard in the lecture. Of course, you might not remember everything about each term, but chances are you can remember *something* about most of them.

Listen for Certain Phrases

As you listen to the lecture for key terms, listen for other signals your teacher gives you that highlight important points that he wants you to know.

Phrases such as, "The most important _____," or "This will be on the test," or "Three key points about _____," indicate the speaker is presenting something worth writing down and reviewing later. Also, throughout any lecture, listen for specific phrases and terms such as "to sum up," "in conclusion," "especially," and "therefore," that indicate a professor is emphasizing a major point.

Step #4: Define and Explain the Key Terms

Write brief explanations or definitions of the key terms next to them, whenever possible. Again, don't write down everything the professor says. Try to jot down just a few words or phrases that will help you remember what a term means later on. If you can't write much about a particular term, don't worry. *Just keep listening and writing!* You'll have plenty of time to fill in more information later. If your professor has moved on to introduce a new topic or key term while you are still taking notes on a previous one, then leave that term behind.

Keeping up with required reading can help when you take notes, as you will feel somewhat familiar with the material already. Key terms from reading assignments are often reinforced in class and vise versa.

You don't need to write perfect, grammatically correct sentences. These notes are written only for you; as long as they make sense to you, nothing else really matters.

Step #5: Develop Your Own Shorthand

Shorthand is a method for writing quickly using shortened versions of words or even symbols. Try to develop your own kind of shorthand; this will enable you to take down more material faster and with less effort. Many study guides teach specific formulas and codes for taking notes in shorthand. The problem with these methods is that you wind up having notes that are practically written in secret code. Don't make your notes overly complicated by developing all kinds of crazy signs and formulas. Find a way to take notes that make sense to you. Here are some basic ways to develop a shorthand that is simple and easy to read.

Avoid Complete Sentences

There's no reason why your notes have to be written in complete, grammatically correct sentences. Sentences are filled with words that aren't necessary for one to understand the gist of them. You can still understand the basic meaning of a sentence without using all the words in it. For example, you can leave out articles (the, a, an) and pronouns (he, she, they, it) and still understand the basic information.

Look at this sentence:

You can omit the articles and pronouns from sentences and still be able to understand them.

You could write it is as:

Omit articles pronouns from sentences still understand

. . . . And you can still gather what was meant.

Keep Descriptions, Examples, and Anecdotes Brief

Very often, your professor will launch into a long description or anecdote as a means of illustrating or explaining some larger point. When the professor does this, you don't necessarily need to transcribe the entire example or anecdote in your notes. You are better off putting down your pen and listening; then write a few key words in your notes to sum up the example or anecdote. Those few words will usually be enough to trigger your memory of the entire explanation. For example, when discussing the classic love tragedy *Romeo and Juliet*, your professor may cite several films or parallels in literature that reflect this same "impossible love" theme. He may show a classical painting depicting tragic lovers, play a clip of the musical *West Side Story*, or even show a clip of the animated film *Gnomeo and*

Juliet to demonstrate how rivalries prevent lovers from being together. Enjoy your professor's examples—resisting writing down word for word what she presents—and then just list the words *West Side Story* or the title and artist of the painting shown to jar your memory of these illustrations at a later date.

Abbreviate Only *Repeated* Key Terms

Using abbreviations is an excellent way to take notes more quickly. If you can reduce words to just a letter or two, it is obviously going to help you write faster. But be very careful. When you abbreviate too many terms, your notes become difficult to read. And if your notes don't make sense to you, then writing more quickly didn't really help you. You should, therefore, only abbreviate key terms that are repeated frequently throughout the lecture.

Use Signs and Symbols

It can also make note-taking much easier if you use signs and symbols for certain commonly repeated words. Again, the idea is to keep it simple. Don't fill up your notes with so many signs that they become impossible to read. Settle on a few common signs that you understand and use all the time. That way, when you read over your notes, you'll know what the signs mean right away without having to think about it.

+	in addition, and
=	equals, is the same thing, is defined as
≠	is not the same thing, is different, unequal
ie	for example
≈	approximately
↗	increases
↘	decreases
⌇↗	has an affect or influence on
→	leads to, results in
@	at or about

✳ or !	this is an important point
vs.	compared to
— —	indicates a new point being raised
;	indicates a closely related point
( )	indicates additional information or a description of a point
⊘	I'm confused about this and need to double-check it

This last sign is very important, as it signals where a problem is and that you need to get more information. Using this circled question mark, you can go on with your note-taking and know you have to come back to that point later. The important thing is not to get stuck on these confusing points—there'll be time to sort them out later, outside of class. Make certain to put the question mark in a circle so that you can distinguish it from other question marks.

Sketch Charts and Diagrams

As the saying goes, a picture paints a thousand words. When it comes to taking notes, drawing a picture is sometimes quicker and more concise than writing detailed explanations. You might, therefore, want to sketch charts and diagrams whenever possible. You don't need to be Picasso to draw a quick, easy-to-read sketch that conveys important information. Just don't overdo it; the purpose of including charts and diagrams is to save time and make your notes easier to understand. If a teacher sketches a portion of your lesson on the board, then by all means try to copy that down in case you are later asked to reproduce and describe parts of it.

ALERT

Don't take notes with different-colored pens or highlighters. Taking notes in different colors can be time-consuming and distracting. While attending class, you should remain focused on the teacher, not on color-coding your notes.

Charts are particularly effective at indicating relationships among terms, people, and concepts. For example, if your professor is telling you about the British royal family, it is much easier to sketch a small family tree that indicates the family's relationships than to continue writing "and Henry married Eleanor and their children were Henry, Edward, and Mathilda, and they married . . ." Charts are also effective when a professor is comparing and contrasting various concepts. You can align the concepts side by side in your notebook to show how they are similar or differ.

Step #6: Construct a Rough Outline

The key terms we've been discussing don't exist in isolation; instead, they are part of a larger structure that is the professor's lecture. Each term ties in to some bigger topic or point being addressed. As you write down those terms, you can begin to construct a rough outline in your notes that will help you see topics they refer to and how various terms are related. Think of the lecture as a puzzle that later, after stepping back from it and absorbing your assignment and how/if it relates to what is presented in class. You can make a more detailed outline outside of class (see Chapter 7 for details on how to do that).

Step #7: Note the General Themes of the Lecture

In most cases, a lecture focuses on a main topic. At the start of the class, you should already have a general idea what this is. Professors who hand out a syllabus or post one online usually list the lecture title with a date beside each. Check your schedule and make certain to see what your teacher has planned for each class. The day's required reading can also give you a sense of what the lecture will address.

Knowing the main topic is an important factor. As you take notes, remember that they all somehow fit in with this topic. Try to figure out what each new piece of information has to do with it. Some pieces may be central to the topic, while others may be less important. In your outline, indicate those that are more central to the main topic.

Within that main topic, there will be several additional topics your professor wants to address or points she wants to make. Here are a few tricks to figuring out what the most important points are within any given lecture:

- **Note what's repeated.** Anything your professor says more than once is going to be important or it wouldn't be worth repeating. Make certain you put a star next to it and/or underline it, to signal that this is a very important point.
- **Watch body language and listen for tone of voice.** Watch and listen more carefully to your professor to see what additional information you can discover from his verbal and nonverbal cues. He might speak more slowly and clearly to emphasize a major point. Many teachers take off their glasses, for example, to emphasize a key point or make eye contact and speak directly to a student.
- **Focus on endings and beginnings.** The end of a lecture is the most important few minutes; this is when most professors re-emphasize or summarize the main points. Don't be one of those students who walks out of class the second that time is up. For one thing, it's rude to the professor and makes a bad impression; but most importantly, you risk missing the most crucial information of the class period.

A Word on Seminars: Taking Notes on Discussions

Until now, you have learned how to take notes during a lecture. These are classes where most of the time is spent listening to a professor speaking, imparting information oftentimes (but not always) to larger classrooms or auditoriums full of students. In addition to lectures, many of your classes might be seminars, where students participate in smaller group discussions led by the professor, an upperclassman, or graduate student Teaching Assistant (T.A.). Discussions can sometimes happen before, after, or during a lecture, as well.

When taking notes during seminars or discussions, your concerns are somewhat different than in lectures. Discussions in seminars are less oriented toward key terms and much less structured. Often they are an opportunity to review and flesh out ideas that may have been less clear from the professor or reading. Here are some suggestions on how to gather the most important information from them in an organized fashion.

Listen More/Write Less and Participate

Since the discussion will be open, feel free to sit back and listen more. By following the discussion carefully, you'll learn a great deal; it won't necessarily be important for you to document everything that is said. These settings are also opportunities for you to speak and participate in the dialogue of the class (if there is one). Your ideas can be discussed, debated and exchanged in seminars more easily than in larger lectures.

Look for Key Terms

Even in a discussion, key terms may come up. You can feel comfortable sitting back and listening, but watch out for them. Whenever the professor introduces new terms, make certain you write them down.

Note Topics of Discussion

Rather than write down everything that everyone says, note only the various topics that come up for discussion. What some other student thinks or feels about a given topic may help you understand the subject better, but you don't need to keep track of it in your notebook. No professor is going to test you on what another student thinks. Having a record of the various topics that were covered in the seminar or small group discussion section gives a good sense of the kinds of topics you may be asked to discuss on an exam.

Note the Professor's Opinions

Your fellow students' opinions about material might not help on an exam, but your professor's views certainly might. After all, the professor is the one who makes the exams. Knowing how she thinks or feels about a topic can indicate what to emphasize in your preparation. When the professor speaks, listen to what she says and take notes. If the professor is expressing an opinion, just write, "Prof. thinks . . ."

QUOTE

"In high school I took notes on whatever piece of paper I had at the bottom of my messy backpack. Sometimes I lost it and never saw it after that day I wrote my notes. Back then I could get by easier with serious listening and borrowing friends' notes. In college, it is a whole other ballgame. I have had to teach myself new techniques and ways to take notes that I can use to review for midterms and exams. I have a notebook for each subject and a system of tabs and post-its I have developed. The best thing I did for myself as a college student was to master a system that works for me."

—Joel T., Freshman

CHAPTER 7

Taking Notes Outside of Class

Some students believe that taking notes occurs only in the classroom when a teacher speaks and presents a lecture. Once you see the value of also taking notes *outside* of class—when you review your in-class notes and read your texts—your mastery of the course content and overall themes and topics will be much greater. Note-taking outside of class completes the circle that connects your in-class lectures and discussions with your outside reading, assignments, and test preparation.

Refining and Adding to Your Notes

You might be thinking to yourself, *aren't we done with note-taking already?* Most students don't review their notes until exam time, only to find they can't make sense out of much of what they've written. This produces a last-minute panic before the exam, as they struggle to relearn an entire semester's worth of material in a few days. Instead of waiting until the last minute to figure out what you've got in your notes, you should get in the habit of working with them outside of the classroom.

After class is over, go back and review your notes while they are fresh in your head either later that day or evening. Any gaps or questions you may have should be addressed right away by asking a classmate or even the teacher about a point that you missed or was confusing. Use your textbook or readings as reference to fill in extra ideas that relate to your notes. That way, you will have more complete outlines from which to study when testing or final exams occur.

Here are some specific steps to take to refine your notes after class:

1. Read over your notes
2. Construct an outline
3. Ask yourself questions
4. Make notes on your notes
5. Go to other sources
6. Fill in additional information
7. Rewrite your notes (optional)

This method will relieve a lot of the pressure if you think you have to get down everything during a lecture. There's another major benefit to following this strategy: The extra attention you devote outside of the classroom guarantees that you better understand your own notes. This means that when exam time comes around, you won't have to panic because you don't remember—or worse, don't understand—things you learned earlier in the semester. Let's look at each step in more depth.

Step #1: Read Over Your Notes

Read your notes over at least once outside of class. This serves two very important purposes:

1. It gives you an opportunity to clarify anything that might be confusing.
2. It helps you learn the information and develop a comfortable familiarity with the whole subject.

If you continue reading over your notes, you'll become more and more immersed in your subject. When the exam comes, you'll feel like you have the information well at hand. Questions won't shock you because they seem alien; instead, you can craft more educated responses.

Make reading over your notes a part of your study habits. You don't need to spend a great deal of time doing this—one or two hours a week per subject should be plenty of time. It's a good idea to do this on Friday or the weekend, so you can look at all your notes for the week. You don't have to read over your notes each night; in fact, sometimes you're better off leaving them alone for a few days. Once you have done your immediate review while the notes are fresh in your mind, then you can leave them alone for a few days. That way, you can approach them with fresh eyes and a clearer head when you do revisit them.

Step #2: Construct a Rough Outline

Don't get stressed out at the idea of making an outline. You may be thinking that outlines are real headaches, that they are overly complicated and don't help all that much. The reason you feel that way is probably because you've been taught that there's only one way to make an outline and that it's a complex matter, with Roman numerals and letters. You don't have to worry about any of that. Making an outline for your notes means crafting a simple diagram that helps you to keep track of how various points and topics are related.

For this outline, group terms together so that you can see how they relate to one another and fall within specific topics and sub-topics. The best way to do this is by skipping lines between topics, and indenting terms beneath the blank lines to show that those terms are part of the topic.

Write a heading that describes each new topic in a few words, and underline it. Enter key terms as they come up by indenting them, about an inch in from the left-hand margin, beneath the topic heading. Doing so indicates the term is a part of the topic above it. You can keep indenting as much as you like to indicate various subtopics and sub-subtopics. In general, the more you indent a term from the margin, the less important it is relative to the main topic.

Here is how a rough outline, without any Roman numerals or letters, might look for a typical lecture:

<u>MAIN TOPIC OF THE LECTURE</u>
(centered and underlined at top)

<u>TOPIC A (The first topic the teacher raises)</u>
  —Subtopic of Topic A (each new topic introduced with a dash)
  —Another Subtopic of Topic A

<u>TOPIC B (The next topic the teacher raises)</u>
  —Subtopic of Topic B
  —Another Subtopic of Topic B
  —Another Subtopic of Topic B
    —A Sub-Subtopic of B
    —Another Sub-Subtopic of B

Remember, It's a *Rough* Outline and It's *Your* Rough Outline

One reason students resist creating outlines in their notes is because they think the professor has some specific outline in her own notes that they need to replicate exactly. It may be true that she does have such an outline, but you don't have to imitate it. The important thing is to take notes that make sense to you.

A good professor will make the organization of the lecture very clear, identifying new topics and important points, as well as the examples and subpoints.

If Your Professor Jumps Around a Lot

Not all professors are organized lecturers, though. Many will stray from whatever the topic is or whatever point they are making to discuss something else. This is known as a *digression*. When a professor digresses, just keep taking notes, but put them in parentheses to indicate they are digressive.

Some professors ramble on, without any clear organization to their points. They may fail to identify new topics, and jump back and forth randomly between points. In these cases, do the best you can. Keep taking notes and don't worry about keeping an outline. Later, try to see connections and relationships between various topics and key terms, and then indicate them in your notes. The thing to keep in mind is that this is just a rough sketch.

Here's something else that should put your mind at ease: You don't necessarily have to have a rough outline at all! Your priority is still to get down the key terms.

Step #3: Ask Yourself Questions

Don't read over your notes with a passive eye. You won't learn anything if you simply read without thinking about what you are reading. Instead, become as involved in your notes as you can. You can do this by considering these questions as you read:

- What does this mean? Does it make sense?
- How are these terms and topics related to one another?
- How do these terms and topics fit into the big picture?

Think of your notes like clues into what your teacher believes is important in his course. The notes you take in class make connections not only to your outside reading assignments but also to the professor's point of view regarding the content. Think of your notes as pieces of a puzzle; the more you try to connect them, the more complete a picture you will get. Each lecture fills in the inside pieces to arrive at a complete message or class concept. Reviewing and trying to make connections between your notes and class content helps you solve the puzzle as you go, sometimes well before the exam date.

Step #4: Take Notes on Your Notes

If you have drawn a line down each sheet of notes, you should have a blank column to the left of the margin. You can now use this space to take notes on your notes. As you ask yourself the above questions, jot down answers here. If something confuses you, make a note of it.

You can also begin to make connections between various topics and terms in this space. During class, you might have tried to put your notes in a rough outline form. As you read over them, other relationships might become clear and you can adjust your outline as necessary. Since you are no longer in class in the middle of a lecture, you now can step back, think, analyze, make connections, and have a sense of the whole topic. You know where your professor is heading with the material. You have a better understanding of what information is important and what doesn't matter as much. Jot down these thoughts in that left-hand margin.

Remember also that you only took notes on one side of the page in class. You can use the back side now to jot down additional notes if you run out of room in the left-hand column.

Step #5: Go to Other Sources

When you're finished reading over your notes, you should have marked areas or written down things that confuse you. Rather than letting those things go and praying they won't be on an exam, you should now take the time to figure them out.

Many people assume that the only source for information for class notes is the professor. That means you are entirely dependent on that one person for all the information. It's not totally realistic to assume the only way you can get clarification is by going to the professor. That view is not really fair to the professor and it's not fair to you. No one can communicate everything in a way that's entirely clear to every person. In addition, some professors are much better at communicating than others. At the same time, you've got to take some responsibility for your own education. You can't just sit back and rely on someone else to do all the work for you. So, if something confuses you, try to educate yourself. There are several places where you can get help, and you can usually get it quickly and easily. Following are some ideas.

What if different sources offer conflicting ideas?
If you come across sources that differ in perspective, go to your teacher or professor to share your discovery. Discuss with them how to address these differing viewpoints. Teachers welcome this kind of inquiry and discovery as you research. Your findings could even contribute to making a paper or class discussion more interesting.

Borrow a Friend's Notes

No two people take exactly the same notes. There's a good chance that someone else caught something you missed during a lecture. If you have gaps in your notes or don't understand a section of your notes, look at a friend's notes. There's absolutely nothing wrong with sharing notes with a friend. Just make certain the friend is a reliable note-taker. You don't want to borrow notes from someone who doesn't take decent notes; you might wind up copying down incorrect information. If you know someone who seems to you like a smart student and efficient note-taker, however, you can begin to exchange notes on a regular basis if she is willing.

Don't rely exclusively on one friend's notes when you miss class. It may be in your best interest to copy notes from at least two classmates to merge their ideas and what they have collected. Often what one student thinks is important is overlooked or not included in another student's notes.

Check Your Textbook

Your textbook for the course and any other required reading materials are valuable resources. More often than not, the required reading assignments you do outside of class relate to the lectures. These may cover many of the same topics and key terms discussed in the lecture. In a lecture, your comprehension is dependent on your listening skills, but in a textbook, where there is a written explanation laid out on the page, you have plenty of time to try to make sense of the material.

Check the index of the textbook for a listing of the topic or key terms for which you want more information. The text's discussion of it may not necessarily be in the same chapter you read for homework. By checking the index, you'll be able to see all the pages in the book where the term is mentioned. For all you know, there is an excellent definition and description of a term in a chapter that's not assigned for reading.

Find More Sources

Sometimes the textbook may still be rather confusing and not give all of the information you need. You might, therefore, want to turn to other sources. By reading an explanation somewhere other than your textbook, you might begin to get a better understanding of the term. In general, the more explanations and interpretations you read, the more complete an understanding you gain.

Other textbooks are places to find more information. You don't have to buy another textbook, although you may want to if it will be helpful. Many school libraries have several textbooks in the reference section. You also need not limit your research to textbooks. Go to the library and look for other books on the subject. If you need suggestions for books and articles to examine, check your textbook to see if there is a bibliography (list of sources used in the book) or a list of suggested additional reading.

You can also check the library search engine or online catalog for other books on that topic. You don't necessarily have to go in search of a specific source; you can simply go to the section of the library where that particular subject is shelved and browse. You'll be amazed at the kinds of things you find. Very often you will get lucky and find a book that covers the course topics clearly and concisely. There may even be a study guide with beautifully written summaries of all the topics you're researching. As you browse, check the tables of contents and indexes for the terms that confuse you. Don't forget to ask the librarian for guidance—she's there to help you and may know of even more resources to check.

You can also go to a major bookstore with academic and scholarly sources, such as campus or chain bookstores, and browse. Many stores sell study guides for all of the main core or fundamental academic subjects taught in high school and college.

ALERT

When referencing sources, err on the side of caution. Some teachers are sticklers on referencing all the information you find elsewhere and can hit you with plagiarism accusations if you don't cite all of your sources. You should even cite Internet search results.

The Internet is another valuable resource for getting information. Online access can provide you with all kinds of supplemental materials that can help increase your understanding. Search engines will pull up many sources for you, including Wikipedia. Just be very cautious that the sites you visit are legitimate, academic-based sites written by professionals and experts.

Ask the Professor

If you are having real trouble understanding an important issue, feel free to go see the professor during office hours. In fact, going to see your professor a few times a semester is a good idea. That way the professor gets to know you by name and you give the impression of being a student who cares about the subject and your education.

Don't overdo it, however. Asking the professor for extra help—either by raising your hand in class or going to his office—might seem like the best way to get a quick and easy explanation of something that confuses you, but it isn't always. For one thing, there's no guarantee he will provide any better an explanation outside of class than he did inside of it. Another problem is that if you always rely on your professor for explanations, you give the impression that you cannot think for yourself. You don't want a professor to have that picture of you in mind when he assigns your grade. A better idea is to try to figure it out yourself and then bring your results to the professor, who can verify or clarify your research as needed.

Step #6: Fill In Additional Information

As you go about your additional research, make certain you take notes and fill in missing information in your notebook. If you found an explanation or definition that helps, write it in your notes. Use the space on the left side of the margin or the back of the sheet. You can also take notes on additional sheets and add them to the notes for that day's lecture if you use a loose-leaf notebook/binder.

Step #7: Rewrite Your Notes (Optional)

With the method that has been outlined here, your notes may have become disorganized and messy, especially as you've added information from other sources. In this case, you may want to rewrite them. You may, for example, want to incorporate the information from the left side of the margin into the notes on the right side. If you have the time, by all means go ahead and do it. If not, what you have already done is probably sufficient. There is no need for overkill.

ESSENTIAL

If your notes are sloppy, take time to rewrite or clean them up. While it may be tedious to go through the rewrite process, it will save you headaches later. Don't wait until the last minute to try to make your notes legible. As you re-examine and research your notes, you may develop a much better understanding of how various topics and terms are related. You may see that certain points go together and connect in a certain way, while others belong somewhere else or are not as important. If this has happened, you may want to rewrite your notes with a new rough outline that makes more sense to you. This may include information in a very different way than you professor delivered it in class. But that's fine. The important thing is that your notes now make sense to you.

Some people believe in rewriting all their notes no matter what. They go home each night and do it meticulously in another notebook. That's pretty much a waste of time and paper. Rewriting doesn't help at all if you haven't really read and thought about the notes, and worked to try to understand them.

How Your Revised Notes Benefit You

If you've followed the method just outlined, both inside and outside of the classroom, you will have accomplished a great deal and acquired knowledge. Not only will you have notes that accurately represent the lectures, you'll also have begun to process the material, making it part of your general knowledge. As you will discover, this useful foundation you have built will make preparing for exams much less stressful for you than for most of your classmates.

The important thing to remember about notes is that they are never really finished products. Most students think their notes are done when the lecture is over. This thinking creates problems that come back to haunt them at exam time. These students open their notebooks and find they can't make heads or tails out of much of what they wrote. Moreover, they have to struggle to memorize these notes as if they are seeing them for the first time.

QUESTION

How should I get notes if I miss a class?
Instead of simply copying a classmate's notes when you miss class, ask someone to tape record the class for you as well. Then you can use the shared notes *and* write notes of your own while listening to the lecture.

Nothing says you can't go back to reread and add to your notes well after a lecture, either. While this should be done each week for that week's notes, you can keep going back to these notes throughout the semester. As you learn new information, in lectures and reading, you may think back on previous information. You may make connections between different points from different lectures, and in the process, may also gain a greater understanding of earlier information.

This note-taking process reflects an accurate view of how learning takes place. You don't learn by ingesting entire blocks of information in one gulp. The mind processes information over time. As you hear and read and discover new information, your mind connects it with previous information. What you didn't understand before may suddenly click into place. As you gain more understanding of something, you make it a part of your overall knowledge. That means it stays with you for long periods of time—right through an exam and beyond.

IMPORTANT NOTE-TAKING POINTS TO REMEMBER

- Effective note-taking starts with effective listening.
- You don't have to write down everything the teacher says; in fact, you shouldn't even try to.
- Notes aren't finished when you leave the classroom; you should continue working with them and thinking about them. This will help you learn the material and save time studying for exams later on.
- You don't need to rely on what the teacher says as your only source of information; feel free to consult other sources for additional information or to clarify points that confuse you.
- Develop your own shorthand for taking notes quickly. Just make certain your notes make sense to you.
- Maintain a sense of the overall topic of each lecture and note general themes.

This note-taking system can transform your classroom experience, if you choose to follow all or parts of it, by making your reading and lectures have more of a purpose and providing you with a clearer understanding of the focus of your assignments. If you have another system that works better for you, than by all means follow that. These ideas and suggestions can serve as both a supplement to and an overhaul of how you have taken notes up until now.

Save Your Old Notes

Many students are so relieved when the semester is over they throw away all their notes. That's a serious mistake. You've worked hard taking those notes! And, more importantly, you never know when you might need to refer back to them. Be a packrat. You never know what you will need again. Be assured that many of the courses you take will interconnect, particularly those within your major or concentration. As you move on to more advanced levels of coursework, you'll find you need to refer to notes from earlier courses to refresh your memory about certain key points or fundamentals.

You also may take courses that seem completely unrelated to one another, only to find that some point or issue will come up that you have previously addressed elsewhere. For example, you may be reading a novel in an English class that refers to specific events from your history class. If you've taken a history class about that period, you can read your notes and get more information about those events, which in turn can help you understand the novel and allow you to contribute more to class discussions. Imagine how impressed your teacher will be if, in class discussion, you can provide some of that background information. So save your notes!

Here's how to keep old notes organized. At the end of the semester, neatly label and put each set of notes someplace safe and accessible. Consider purchasing a file cabinet to store them in or large clear plastic containers you can easily buy at an office supply store. If you've been using a loose-leaf notebook, you can take the pages out of the binder and put them in a folder. That way you can reuse the binder next semester. Just make certain you label the folder with the course title and year.

In addition to saving old notes, consider holding on to some of your required textbooks and other course materials. It's tempting at the end of the semester to sell all your books back to the bookstore—especially given how expensive books are these days. If there is any chance you will refer to a book—particularly if it was used in a course that is part of your major—it is probably worthwhile to hold on to it. One option is to sell only the textbooks and keep all other books. Textbooks tend to be more expensive than other books, and you get back a significant amount of money. Other books often bring only a fraction of the original cost (especially if they are paperbacks).

QUOTE

"My roommate had it all figured out when it came to note-taking. It never dawned on me to look at my notes *after* class was over. I believed that note-taking was something I did only when a professor spoke to me. Once I watched her master the course content and be able to explain it to me, she shared with me her secret: taking notes outside of class, too. She showed me her process and now I make better connections between my lectures and outside class work. It really works!"

—Sandra L., Junior

CHAPTER 8

Reading Texts

Reading texts can be an active or passive experience, similar to determining your behavior inside class as an active or passive listener. Furthermore, taking notes when you read from a text is different than classroom note-taking. Reading texts requires a more concentrated focus since the words themselves are teaching you, rather than a live person at the front of a classroom. Reading textbooks and other required sources is a major part of the educational process. Yet many students go about their reading in completely the wrong way. Here's how to do it the right way!

Types of Poor Readers

Students who do not read their text effectively come up with many ways to do it incorrectly. Here are some profiles of types of readers you may find familiar.

"Highlighter Happy" Students

Some students are "highlighter happy," tackling a required reading assignment by using a bright yellow highlighter as a machete. As they read, they highlight anything that looks remotely important, could be worth remembering, might be on a test, or is confusing. When a highlighter-happy student's mind starts to wander, she doesn't really worry; as long as something is highlighted, she believes she has "covered" it. When highlighter-happy people are done reading, more of the page is bright yellow rather than white. They are satisfied with their work, certain that they have read the chapter thoroughly.

Unfortunately, these students are often surprised when they do poorly on the final exam. And that's not the worst of it. When they try to sell back their fifty-dollar textbook at the end of the semester, the bookstore won't take it. All that the clerk asks is, "Who wants to buy a neon yellow textbook?"

Bored Readers

Some students find reading boring. The title of a book alone can put them to sleep or in a foul mood. A bored reader scans the first few sentences, comes across terms he's never seen before, like "signifier" and "syntax," and begins to roll his eyes. "This is soooo boring," he thinks to himself. He reads another line, and then glances out the window, staring at the sky, trees, and a dog catching a Frisbee on the grass, then he returns to read the assignment. He has forgotten now what he just read since his mind was wandering moments before, so he starts reading from the beginning. Rubbing his aching head, he reads the first two paragraphs, and soon begins to think about his weekend plans. What will he do Saturday night? He then goes back to the reading, but once again has lost his place. He starts the first sentence again, then decides the reading is just too boring and probably won't be on the test anyway. Unfortunately, he is wrong.

Speed Readers

Finally, there are the speed readers, who look over the syllabi for their fall courses, realize that to do all the required reading for their five courses will take about forty hours a week. Then they realize that to do all that reading is practically impossible if they are also going to attend classes, eat, and sleep.

ALERT

Be wary of thinking you have mastered speed-reading. By definition, skipping over words means you are overlooking content, sometimes crucial content. If you speed-read and still have success mastering concepts and earning good grades, then continue. Otherwise, good old-fashioned focused reading will do the trick.

On the side of a bus, a student might see what she thinks is her salvation, an advertisement for a course in Super Speed-Reading. She pays $500 for a three-hour seminar on super speed-reading, given at a local motel. In the course, she learns to run her fingers down the page as fast as she can, reading just the middle section of each line. The instructor assures the class that although they may feel they are missing a great deal, the brain still manages to process everything it sees, even at this speed. A proud graduate of the course, the speed reader can now read the "Semiology" article at a super-speed, finishing it in four and a half minutes—without understanding a word of it!

Getting Started

We all think we can read fairly well; after all, most of us have been doing it since elementary school. But reading serious academic texts is much more difficult than the other kinds of reading we are accustomed to. It requires a whole new set of skills and techniques.

The reading strategy outlined in this chapter involves taking notes while you read. You might, therefore, want to read at a desk or table as opposed to lying down on a bed or couch; if not, bring some kind of flat surface (a large hardcover book, clipboard, or lap desk) on which to write. You'll also need the same loose-leaf paper you use for taking notes in class. Make certain to write the date and author or title of the material you are reading at the top of each page. That way, if the sheets get out of order, you can easily put them back. After each reading assignment, when you're done taking notes, put them in the same notebook binder where you keep your classroom notes.

ESSENTIAL

If your professor has assigned a reading for a particular day, bring your notes from your reading with you to the lecture; this will enable you to refer to them and fill in any gaps on the fly you may encounter.

If your reading assignments don't coordinate with the lectures, keep reading notes in a separate section of your binder. Usually, however, your professor coordinates reading assignments with lectures. If this is the case, keep the reading notes alongside the lecture notes. By keeping lecture and reading notes side by side, you'll be able to observe the ways in which the reading assignments and lectures fit together and relate to one another. For example, you'll see if certain points are covered repeatedly —an indication they are especially important and likely to show up on an exam.

Effective Reading: A Step-by-Step Strategy

In order to become an *effective* reader, you have to be an *active* reader. That means doing more than just looking at the words on the page; it means becoming involved with the material and *thinking* while you read. Here are some strategies for effective reading of academic materials. The goal for note-taking while reading a text is the same as the goal for note-taking in the classroom: to become a more active learner who absorbs and understands the information being conveyed.

These are the basic steps of the strategy:

1. Know where you're headed—and why
2. Make a rough outline
3. Watch for key terms and take notes with brief definitions
4. Note general themes
5. Write a response

In the detailed description of the steps that follow, you will learn more effective ways to read a textbook. Most courses you take require you to use a textbook that has been written for that subject, especially in the survey and introductory courses you take in high school or as a college underclassman.

Step #1: Know Where You're Headed—and Why

When you go on a trip, you usually have an itinerary that maps out your destination and the route you will take to get to it. You know exactly where you are going and why—and that's what keeps you from getting lost. The same holds true for reading assignments. If you don't want your mind to wander, make certain you know right from the beginning where you're headed and the route you are taking. Before you begin reading, think a bit about *what* you are reading. What is the title of the chapter, article, or text? Does it give you any hint as to what you can expect? As with classroom lectures, each chapter or article you read will have a main topic. Make certain you know the topic before you start to read.

Try to keep in mind not only *what* you are reading, but *why*. Of course, one reason is because the material is required reading. But if that is the only reason, you are going to get bored pretty quickly and resentful of your homework assignment and that can lead to you "tuning out." Each chapter assigned somehow contributes to your understanding of the course material, as well as to your general knowledge. If you can designate a purpose for each thing you read, you'll feel better about doing the work and achieving a deeper understanding of it. You won't be reading just to please the professor, but because you see some value in fulfilling the assignment.

Keep these questions in mind when you are reading:

- What do you think your professor is hoping you will gain by reading this?
- What might you personally gain from this reading assignment?
- How does the chapter or text fit in with the overall subject matter of the course?
- How does the text fit in with the current course topics (i.e., the lectures for that week)?
- Does the chapter build on previous material? How?
- Does the chapter prepare you for upcoming topics? How?
- Is anything in the chapter familiar to you? What? Where and when did you first learn it? What did you already learn? What in the chapter is new to you?

Thinking about these questions helps you become actively involved in the reading assignment right from the start. These questions also help you gain a more personal interest in the reading by connecting it with your overall knowledge. That way, you won't feel you are reading just because it's required, but because it can somehow enhance your understanding of the subject matter.

Step #2: Make a Rough Outline

Just as you do when taking notes during a lecture, make a rough outline of most reading assignments. If an assignment is creative—e.g., an art project —or simply an analysis of a text, for example, don't feel that you have to takes notes on that assignment, too. Use your judgment on what seems a worthwhile way to spend your time. Not all students need to take notes on everything. If you choose to take notes on your reading, this will fulfill two important purposes:

1. Taking notes gives you something to *do* while you read, making you more of an *active* reader with a purpose. This, in turn, keeps you focused on the assignment and minimizes the tendency to let your mind wander.
2. These outlines help you remember the material.

When it comes time to study for an exam, you can read over these notes rather than having to go over large, highlighted chunks of text in a book.

FACT

A rough outline can be a useful tool to serve as a sort of "SparkNotes" for your reading assignment. With multiple assignments and subjects to juggle, referring to a rough outline can be enough to jog your memory about the content of an assignment when they risk merging together and being forgotten.

To make the rough outline, just note various topics and subtopics as you did with lecture notes. Making a reading outline will be easier than taking notes during a lecture since most textbooks (unlike some professors) make it very clear how they are organized. Many books list, either in the table of contents or at the start of the chapter beneath the title, the topics covered in a particular chapter. Within a chapter, the topics, subtopics, and sub-sub-topics usually have clearly labeled headings and subheadings. Most books differentiate between the more important topics and lesser ones by changing the typeface style of the headings. For example, the more important headings will be larger and/or in boldface, while less important ones will be smaller and in lighter or italic type. As you read, watch for headings and subheadings and, as they come up, write them down. As with any outline, the less important a topic is, the more you indent its location on your paper.

Step #3: Watch for Key Terms

Most textbook chapters also center on key terms—names, dates, facts, theories, and concepts—that are new to you. And just as you take notes in lectures, look for key terms and include them in your reading notes. It will probably be easier to identify these terms in textbooks than during lectures because in most textbooks they are in boldface or italics. Try to fit them into your rough outline by placing them beneath the same heading or subheading in your notes as they appear in the chapter.

Include brief definitions of these key terms. You don't need to write these definitions in complete sentences. Use abbreviations and symbols.

Just remember, though, that your notes should still be easy for you to read. Don't copy down the exact, word-for-word explanation of the term as you find it in the text. Instead, use your own words and paraphrase to define the term as briefly as possible.

Step #4: Note General Themes

When you are finished with a chapter, take a few minutes to jot down its general themes. To help you identify these, consider the following questions:

- What seemed to be the author's main concerns in this chapter?
- What ideas, topics, or points were mentioned more than once?
- Was there any kind of introduction or conclusion? If so, what points did the author make here?
- Did you get a sense of the author's opinion or stance on the material he or she was addressing? What was it?

These notes will be instrumental in helping you prepare for exams. In addition to helping you recall the overall content of a reading assignment, your notes will enable you to compare the key themes of all reading assignments and classroom lectures. This process will help you gain a sense of how various parts of the course fit together. And it's a safe bet that when themes show up throughout the semester, they're likely to appear on an exam.

Step #5: Write a Response

The reading process doesn't end when you get to the last word of the chapter. When students complete the last sentence of a reading assignment, many think, "Whew! That's finished. What a relief!" and close the book without giving it another thought. They don't realize that a great deal of the work they've just done will have been a waste of time. While they have read the assignment, they have not really *thought* about it.

They have looked at the words on the page, but they haven't thought about what they mean. They don't know if they even understood what they have just read. In short, they haven't really learned anything based on what they've read. If you want to learn something from what you read, it is crucial that you *think* about it after you've finished reading. An excellent way to keep you thinking is to write a reading response.

To write a reading response, simply write whatever you want about what you've read. A reading response is *not* a summary of the chapter. Instead, it's your opportunity to engage with the material you've just read. Think of yourself as having a conversation with the author of the text. This is your chance to share whatever is on your mind.

Here are some questions you might address in your response:

- What is your emotional reaction to what you've read? Do you like what you read? Why or why not? How did reading the text make you feel? How do you think the writer wants you to feel?
- What points do you think are most important to the writer? Did the writer successfully convey these to you?
- What parts, if any, did you have trouble understanding? Why? What made it confusing?
- What questions about the text do you still have? Make certain you list questions about any terms, topics, or points you didn't understand. You can also list questions you have that arise from the reading. Are there any additional questions about the subject matter that were not addressed in the text? (By the way, these questions don't necessarily have to be answered right away. They may be answered as you read more throughout the semester; or, they may never be answered.)
- How does this text connect with other concepts you've learned? Does it tie into ideas you've studied in other courses? Does the reading remind you of anything else?

Even though you write the responses *after* you finish reading, writing them is going to help you become a more effective reader and active participant in the reading process. Many students approach required readings like mindless robots; they focus on the words on the page and try to suppress any of their own thoughts or feelings. But the mind wants to be more involved than that. And if it's not involved, it is going to wander. You are not a robot. You are a real person who has thoughts, feelings, and opinions about what you read. You are allowed to like something you read, or to dislike it. Your reading might either confuse or excite you. Your response gives you the opportunity to express what you are thinking and feeling. As you become more used to this process, you'll find yourself considering your thoughts about a reading assignment as you read it.

Follow Up

Once a week, set aside time to read over your responses to the reading assignments for the previous week. Pay special attention to any questions you had about things you did not understand, and make note of them in the margins. You can then go to other sources for more detailed explanations of these tricky concepts, just as you did for your lecture notes. You can look up the subject online. You can also ask friends in the class or the professor about difficult points you don't understand.

ALERT

Review. Review. Review. Go back and review old notes from time to time as well as your reading responses to gain a better understanding of how your course has progressed. Sometimes you will have an "a-ha moment" when the ideas start to come together and make more sense to you.

You may want to read your written responses throughout the semester, especially as you get closer to an exam. You'll find that as a course progresses and you get deeper into the subject matter, you'll gain a better understanding of key concepts and some of your responses will start to either make sense or not pertain to the overall class concept at all. You'll also start to see how different concepts are related to one another, and how they fit into the "big picture" of the course. A reading assignment that initially confused you may make sense later in the semester. Long after you've completed a reading, you might begin to see how the material relates to another reading or topic covered in class. You can then go back over your initial response and make additional notes that indicate what you now understand.

Be a Selective Reader, Not a Speed-Reader

You are probably going to have many more reading assignments than you can possibly read. For many students, the solution is to take a course, or buy a book, on speed-reading. Speed-reading, though, is perhaps the most passive form of reading there is. Most speed-reading methods encourage you to flip pages as fast as possible by reading only small sections of the text, such as the middle column on the page. The advocates of these methods claim that you do, in fact, comprehend everything you read this way, and that as long as your eye sees words on the page, you can "read" them.

The problem with this method is that you don't have the opportunity to think about what your eye sees. And if you don't think about the material, you are not going to absorb it. That means it can be all too easily forgotten. You probably won't be able to use the assigned reading material to answer questions on an exam.

How to Skim a Text

Rather than not read a text at all, you may decide to skim it. Skimming a text doesn't mean you just read it at a slightly faster pace than usual. It is really a form of selective reading.

The best way to skim a text is to do the following:

1. **Read introductions, conclusions, and summary paragraphs.** You should read the introduction and conclusion of each text in their entireties, as these paragraphs usually outline the most important points covered in the text. You might also look for "summary paragraphs." These are paragraphs within the text that summarize smaller sections of the text rather than the whole thing. If a text is divided into topics and subtopics, each with its own heading, these sections might have their own introductions and conclusions. As you skim, be on the lookout for terms such as, "in conclusion," "to sum up," and "therefore," that indicate the author is summarizing various points.

2. **Read first and last lines of paragraphs.** If you go through a text and read just the first and last line of each paragraph, you will actually get an adequate concept of what the text covers. The first line of many paragraphs will introduce the topic covered, while the last line will often summarize

the contents of the paragraph or serve as a transition to the next paragraph. As you read first and last sentences, you might come across a line that indicates a paragraph is particularly important or intriguing. If that happens, go ahead and read the entire paragraph.

3. **Look at illustrations.** Just as first and last sentences of paragraphs often sum up key points, pictures, charts, and diagrams usually correspond to key information conveyed in the text. Look over all of these and read the captions that explain them.

4. **Read all words and phrases that are set in boldface or italics.** If the term is unfamiliar to you and seems significant, read the entire sentence as well.

However, don't fool yourself into thinking skimming is a thorough reading. Skimming is just that: lightly going over an assignment and gaining a general overview. It's what to do if you're in a pinch and should not be your overall strategy.

Challenges with Texts

If you are having tremendous difficulty with a particular text, there's no reason why you can't seek help. Here are some places to go.

Other Written Materials

Just as you do for your lecture notes, you can try to find other textbooks and source materials that cover similar topics. Go look at other textbooks, academic encyclopedias, study guides such as Schramm's Outlines or Barron's Guides, and other books on the same general subject. Check the back of the assigned text to see if there is a bibliography, works cited, or list of suggested reading. CliffsNotes or SparkNotes, if used properly as reading supplements, can be effective learning tools to reinforce terms or fill in any gaps or ideas you may have missed or misunderstood along the way.

You might get lucky and find a book or article that covers the exact same material but is written in much simpler language that makes it easier to understand. Even if you find sources that are equally complex, it will probably help to read them. Other sources might describe the same material in a different way. For example, they might use different illustrations and examples to describe the same overall principles. By reading more than one source on the same topic, you could gain a fuller explanation and a more complete understanding of it.

Work Together with Classmates

You can also discuss the reading assignment with fellow students. Since these assignments are not graded, there's no reason why you can't work with friends. Perhaps a fellow student just happens to have a better understanding of this particular subject than you do, and you can ask her questions. It's important, though, that you have a *discussion* with the student about the text rather than just get answers. Express your own opinions and thoughts. Having a conversation ensures that you listen carefully to the other student and also that you think more about the text.

Even if other students don't have a firm grasp on the material, a discussion may help you come to a better understanding of it. Try taking turns attempting to "teach" sections of the text to one another; very often, in the process of trying to explain something to another person, you also manage to explain it better to yourself.

Ask Your Instructor

Finally, you can always ask your instructor for extra help. Only do this if you really need the help and have tried to sort out the problem on your own first. Don't ask for it on every assignment. You don't want to give the impression that you are too lazy to do the work and can't think for yourself. If you do decide to ask for help, see your professor during office hours or after class and say, "I'm having trouble understanding 'Source X.' I wonder if you can recommend some other sources to read that could provide me with more information." By asking for more sources rather than an explanation of the material, you are indicating that you are willing to work on your own. The professor then may, in addition to recommending sources, ask you where you are having trouble and offer further explanations. Whatever you do, do not complain about how hard or boring a reading assignment is—nothing makes a worse impression!

Using Other Sources

So far we've primarily been discussing how to read textbooks. While many college and high school classes rely on textbooks, especially for introductory and survey courses, you will probably be assigned readings from a variety of sources. You can generally follow the reading strategy outlined above, although you may emphasize certain steps more than others, depending on the type of source you read. Here are some typical types of materials you may encounter in high school and college.

Scholarly Articles

These are articles written by professors and academics that appear in professional journals. They are often only a few pages (between five and ten). But don't be fooled by their length; they will often require much more time and effort to read. These are the sources most likely to be written in academic style, using sophisticated vocabulary and addressing complex ideas. The authors of these articles often assume their readers have the same level of education and background as they do. That means they will be less likely to define key terms and concepts for you than a textbook does. You therefore might have to spend more time in the library using other sources to understand the information conveyed.

ALERT

If you find yourself reading the same sentence over and over again, not comprehending it, it's a sure-fire sign you are not focusing. Take a break, get some fresh air, have a snack, stretch. Do whatever you need to do to refresh so you can get back on track and refocus.

Primary Sources

Many courses include primary sources, such as historical documents, novels, plays, etc. It is vital that you read these sources before class so that you can follow the lecture. Primary sources, particularly works of literature, often won't involve key terms and won't necessarily include clearly identifiable introductions and conclusions. Rather than making outlines that include key terms, you need only to note the general themes or characters. You should still write a reading response if you can, as this will help you recall the source in more detail when you study for an exam.

Lab Reports

For science classes, you may be required to read laboratory reports, accounts of experiments, and scientific studies. The most important element to read and make a note of is the outcome of the experiment. But don't be fooled into thinking you only need to read the conclusion. Make certain you have a sense of the general parameters of the experiment, such as the setup of the study and who participated in it.

Also, try to evaluate the study: Are there any flaws in the setup or in the scientists' reasoning? Are there any factors that could have influenced the findings other than the ones the scientists discussed? What are the assumptions that were made in the study? Were the scientists aware of these assumptions? These issues often form the basis for examination questions.

Course Packets

Sometimes the professor puts together a special packet for the course that includes a variety of materials such as articles, charts, diagrams, and excerpts from longer texts. Always read everything in a course packet carefully. If the professor took the time to compile it, it is probably important.

Remember the Big Picture!

The reading assignments you do for your classes are not isolated exercises. Each piece you read is a part of the bigger picture: the particular course or subject. It is also a part of an even bigger picture: your general knowledge. In fact, even the reading you do outside of class contributes to your general knowledge. You learn something from everything you read, whether it's a textbook, novel, or magazine article. Ask yourself what, exactly, are you learning from this piece? How is this text contributing to your overall knowledge? As long as you keep that big picture in view, you'll always be an active and effective reader.

IMPORTANT POINTS TO REMEMBER

- Be an active reader; become involved with what you read.
- For each reading assignment, know where you're headed and why.
- Think while you read and after you read; ask yourself questions and write a response.
- Throw away the highlighters; rely on your own notes about reading assignments.
- Be a selective reader rather than a speed-reader. Prioritize your reading assignments in order of importance. If you can't read the entire assignment, skim it.
- Be willing to work hard on difficult texts; don't use the "boredom" excuse.

QUOTE

"I use my 'free' times or open blocks during my day for a variety of tasks. Sometimes I use it to study, read required texts, or do homework. Other times I reward myself and use free time to eat, relax, or socialize. It depends each day on how my tasks at hand line up, but I made the mistake early on of using free time to just hang out and my grades really suffered. I learned nothing really is 'free' in life!"

—Alan T., Sophomore

CHAPTER 9

Effective Study Skills

You need to adopt an effective study routine for everything you do. As a student, you are faced with many tasks, activities, and responsibilities; it is overwhelming. The key to making it all manageable is making it a matter of habit. The more routine something is, the less effort it requires. Think about your morning routine. You probably go through the same ritual every day—showering, brushing your teeth, and getting dressed—without thinking about it. If you also make study tasks a habit, they'll come as easy as brushing your teeth.

Create an Effective Study Space

Not every student studies and gets work done in the same manner. Some of your classmates may need to come home, decompress, turn on the TV, have a snack, and relax before they get to the grind of homework. Others go straight to extracurricular activities, an after-school job or volunteer work, go home for dinner, and then begin homework once all of that is done. Others use free blocks during the school day to get ahead. Whatever is your style or routine, find a system, time, and way to get your work done that works best for you.

ALERT

Have your eyes checked annually. Reading books up close or gluing your eyes to a computer monitor for hours at a time can strain and affect your eyesight. Find out if reading glasses or resting your eyes periodically can help reduce eyestrain. Keep rewetting or lubricating drops on hand just in case your eyes dry out.

Figure Out What Works for You

Do you prefer quiet solitude in a corner of a library? Do you need your iPod to mask outside distracting dorm sounds when you work? Do you stay on task with a buddy and social component as part of your homework or study routine? Do you prefer to break up your work in smaller chunks or to work subject by subject, immersing yourself into one discipline at a time? Some coursework is more conducive to group or dialoguing when you study. Other subjects require deeper concentration and memorization. Find a strategy that suits your learning style and stay consistent.

The space where you choose to do your work is crucial to your success as a student. Obviously, make sure the space where you do your work is well lit, free from distractions (like a cell phone, computer that could distract you with instant messages or the lure of the Internet and e-mail, or your iPod), and is an environment where you can successfully get your work done. Determine what environment is in its most suitable condition for your academic success. Then discipline yourself to enforce limitations to keep your area in that condition.

ALWAYS do you homework. That is a given. It is expected of you and directly impacts your grade and your understanding of the material significantly.

Many people seem to think that the only way to study is at a bare desk, with a hard-backed chair, in a minuscule cubicle in the library. While this setting does wipe out any outside distraction, it's such a gloomy, sterile atmosphere that it turns studying into a form of medieval torture. Studying doesn't have to be that depressing. Since you will spend long hours at the books, reading over your notes and assigned texts, you may as well make yourself comfortable. If you work in a space where you are relaxed and feel at home, you will study more often and more effectively. Study anywhere you feel comfortable—in your room, in bed, at the library, in an empty classroom, at a café, outside, in the park—provided that you do two things:

1. Minimize outside distractions.
2. Promise yourself to make a change if you don't get the work done.

In choosing a place, consider the amount of outside distraction—such as friends stopping by, the phone ringing, loud music—and do what you can to minimize it. Even the library may not be distraction-free; if everyone you know goes there to study, you may spend more time chatting with friends than studying. You can, though, minimize the distraction by avoiding the main study lounge and finding a quieter section of the library, where you won't run into many people you know.

Adopt the right study habits, since not all habits are necessarily good. Once any habit is set, it becomes hard to break. Good study skills basically come down to this: figure out the best way to memorize and analyze information and do your school work effectively.

There's nothing wrong with studying in your room so long as you get work done. Your room is, after all, the space where you are most at home. Again, minimize distractions. If you are frequently interrupted by the phone, siblings, friends, or instant messaging, turn the ringer or your computer screen off; if friends or siblings frequently disturb you, keep the door closed.

If you decide to study in your room, it's a good idea to designate a spot as your main workspace. Your desk is probably the best place. You can listen to music while you study, just as long as it doesn't distract you. Listening to something old that you are very familiar with will distract you less than newly released tunes that might make you curious to hear the lyrics. If you study outside your room, you can try bringing your iPod along to listen to relaxing music. That's one way to make wherever you study feel a little more like home.

Consider Multiple Spots

You can also designate different places for different study tasks. For example, you might decide to read assignments for class at home, but go over lecture notes in the library. Studying in a variety of locations can make the process less tedious. You should make it a habit, though, to do the same study tasks in the same place so they will seem more routine.

Stay Focused

Sometimes, for whatever reason, you'll find it difficult to pay attention. When this happens, a simple change of scene may be all you need to refocus on your work. If you've been studying at your desk, go out somewhere, to a coffee shop or the library, and see if you get more done.

If you find that you consistently don't get a great deal of work done, however, make a more permanent change. If, for example, you are so relaxed studying in your room that you always fall asleep, then that's probably not ever the best place for you to work.

Staying Awake

Whatever your learning style might be, it is important that you stay awake and alert when you study. It might sound like a joke, but falling asleep while reading or studying is a problem that plagues many students. The need to sleep is powerful—and to fight it, you need to take equally strong measures. Here are a few important suggestions:

- **Get enough sleep at night.** There's a simple reason why so many students fall asleep while studying, and it's not necessarily boredom. They're just tired. Of course, it's difficult when you are a student to get a good night's sleep all the time, and you shouldn't expect to. Don't make a habit of staying up late all the time, though. Try as often as possible to get six to eight hours of sleep a night.
- **Don't get too much sleep.** You might not realize it, but there is such a thing as too much sleep. For most people, six to eight hours of sleep a night is sufficient. If you get more sleep than your body needs, you can feel sleepy all day long.
- **Exercise regularly.** If you exercise regularly, you'll sleep better at night and be more energized during the day. Your blood and brain will get more oxygen and better flow through your body. That means you'll be more alert and focused on your classes and your studies.
- **Become alarmed.** If you tend to fall asleep while studying, set an alarm. You can purchase an inexpensive travel clock or wristwatch equipped with an alarm and have it nearby while you study. Or you can set your cell phone to beep or vibrate in intervals to potentially wake you up. The alarm should be loud enough to wake you but quiet enough not to disturb those around you. If possible, set the alarm to go off every fifteen minutes. If you can't set it to go off regularly, set it for a specific time (such as a half hour after you've begun studying) and continue to reset it each time it goes off.
- **Schedule wake-up calls or visits.** If you don't trust an alarm, have a friend check on you every so often. The easiest method is to arrange to study together; that way you can both keep an eye on the other and keep each other awake. Of course, you have to be careful that you both don't fall asleep at the same time, and also that you don't spend too much time chatting. If you are studying in your room, you can have a friend or relative give you a phone call every hour or stop by from time to time to check on you.

- **Take breathers.** If you become too comfortable while studying, it's easy to fall asleep. You should plan to get up and walk around at regular intervals—preferably outside. While fresh air can do wonders for waking you up, limit your walks to just five minutes. When you return to studying, you'll feel revived and better able to focus. Also, study with your window open, weather permitting.
- **Stay actively involved.** The more engaged in the material you are, the less likely you'll succumb to sleep. Rather than just reading the words on the page, have a conversation with yourself in your mind about what you read; read a few lines and then comment on them.
- **Don't get too comfortable.** It's important to be comfortable while you study because the more relaxed you are, the more open your mind will be. Additionally, being comfortable makes studying less tedious. There is such a thing, though, as being too comfortable. If you find yourself constantly falling asleep, you should change your study habits. Avoid clothing that is too warm, comfortable, or cozy. In other words, don't wear clothes that feel too much like pajamas, which might help lull you to sleep.

Organization Tips

When you're a student, studying becomes your job. But being a student is tougher than some nine-to-five office jobs because your responsibilities and duties are constantly changing. Every day, every week, every month, and every semester present new assignments and tasks, and if you don't keep track of them, you'll find that your work—and your life—become a complete mess.

That's why it's essential that you organize yourself right from the start. We already discussed keeping calendars and schedules in Chapter 5. Here are some other ways to keep yourself and your life organized.

In addition to keeping careful records of your responsibilities in your calendar, you should also keep all of your notes and study materials neatly organized. There's not much point in taking notes if they wind up in a crumpled pile of paper at the back of your desk. Keep your notes clearly labeled and organized. Find a space you can designate as your study area, where you keep all the study materials—notes, textbooks, articles—that you need for the semester. That way you'll be able to quickly find anything you need.

ALERT

Set alarms on your computer's calendar to remind you of upcoming tests or papers. Your alarms can also alert you to teacher office hours, blocks of study time you have in your calendar, or tutorials. Don't try to keep unnecessary information floating around in your head. That's why these devices were invented!

Another way to keep organized is to break down larger projects into smaller pieces. For example, if you have a huge book report and presentation to finish, make a timeline and carve the project into pieces with labeled index cards or computer files with names labeling topics such as: introduction, supporting paragraphs, references and bibliography, project visuals, conclusion, examples and illustrations of text, etc.

Come up with a system that works for you and then repeat it over and over. And fine-tune it along the way if you need to.

Analyzing a Text

Time and again, you will have reading assignments that ask you to analyze a text. Some texts are simply a passage or chapters from a book or novel, others are poetry. Having a basic set of questions to consider and a vocabulary to use when analyzing any text will be helpful to you as you dissect and analyze your reading assignments.

Consider these questions as you read the text:

- What is the language expressing?
- What is the author's tone?
- What is the issue being expressed by the author and how is it being conveyed?
- Are there similes or metaphors used to help convey the author's message? (such as light and darkness, augury [bird symbols], age and youth, etc.)
- How is the text organized?

For a book of fiction:

- What is the plot?
- Who are the main characters and how are characters related or interconnected?
- What symbolism or imagery does the author use?
- From whose point of view is the story told, and how is that point of view stilted or biased to the reader?
- Is there a problem being addressed or question that motivates the character of the story?
- What is your personal reaction to the text? Enjoyment or disgust? Curiosity or indifference?
- Can you personally identify with any of the characters? If so, how?
- What is the main style of writing? Is it descriptive language to present you with images of the setting? Is it dialogue between characters?
- Is there any subtext that is meaningful?

Sometimes you're asked to respond to a particular passage within a text with an innovative idea. How do you discover something new in that quote? Here are some easy guidelines to assist you in expressing your own analysis:

1. Try to provide a summary of your personal opinions about the quote you selected in a sentence or two.
2. Give the reader your reason for selecting that quote to analyze so that the teacher understands the context of your quote (even though most of the time they have read the book).
3. Insert your quotation and follow that up with any additional observations you have about it.

Learning Key Terms

Your teacher will likely identify key terms throughout the course and use them repeatedly. Often you will be tested on key terms, but more importantly, when you use them in your writing assignments, class discussions, quizzes, tests, or exams—it shows your teacher that you understand them. You might even earn extra points for incorporating them into your work for that class. Key terms are essentially "buzzwords" that your teacher hopes you will add to your vocabulary throughout the term. Following are several techniques you can use to learn key terms.

Flash Cards

The most effective way to memorize key terms is to work with good, old-fashioned flash cards. Flash cards are particularly helpful when you need to remember a lot of key terms, such as new vocabulary words in a foreign language. Simply take 3" × 5" index cards and write down a term on one side and either a definition, a description of its significance, or a translation on the other.

Although making the flash cards might seem time-consuming, this method has many advantages.

First, the process of making the cards helps you begin to memorize the material. As you write down a term and its definition, your mind begins to process the information into your long-term memory.

Second, using cards enables you to shuffle and reorganize them in various ways. For example, you can eliminate cards for terms you know well, and continue to test yourself on the ones you don't.

FACT

For common survey courses such as U.S. history, biology, or even geometry, pre-printed flash cards with definitions on the back are sold in bookstores or can be downloaded and printed. If you are not the type who will take the time to write out your own old-fashioned flash cards, consider purchasing these or printing them from the Internet. Making them yourself can improve your mastery of the material, however.

Third, flash cards enable you to quiz yourself both ways: You can look at the term and test yourself on the definition or look at the definition and try to guess the term. If you can do both, then you truly know the material. This can particularly help on those questions where you need to furnish the term yourself, such as with fill-in-the-blank questions. For this reason, flash cards are also useful in preparing for exams on foreign language vocabulary where you need to know either the English definition of a word or the foreign word to answer questions.

Flash cards make it easy for you to test yourself on key terms. Quiz yourself often. Sit with the stack of cards and, for each one, state the definition or description of the term. Then flip the card over to see if you were correct. If you were right and feel pretty confident that you won't forget the term, you can put the card aside. If you got it wrong or had trouble describing it in detail, put the card at the bottom of the stack. Before you do, though, read over the card a few times and make a concentrated effort to remember it. You won't be able to remember something merely because you've read it; you have to make an effort and instruct yourself to remember it.

When you have finished going through the whole stack, shuffle it and start again. Repeat the process, continuing to eliminate any cards you find you know quite well. Eventually you should be able to go through the whole deck and define each term without hesitation. You'll know then that you are ready for the exam.

Improve Your Memory

Some people are gifted with photographic memories. They can read a passage of a text and then repeat it word for word from memory. Most people, though, have a great deal of difficulty memorizing information. Like listening, memorizing takes effort. There are, however, a number of strategies to help you improve your memory. These are known as *mnemonic devices*. Many people think that if they stare at a word, text, or image long enough, they will remember it. They think that by staring at something, they have probably succeeded at inputting the information into their long-term memory.

The trouble comes later on, when they try to retrieve that information. Long-term memory is somewhat like a large clothes closet—it can hold an awful lot but, as you put more and more into it, it becomes harder to pick out exactly what you want. Mnemonic devices function as trigger mechanisms that conjure more detailed information from your long-term memory.

Rhymes

Ancient storytellers who didn't know how to read or write could recite epic-length poems completely from memory. They depended on rhythm, alliteration, and especially rhyming words to help trigger their memories of the entire work. For example, if they could remember the first line of a rhymed couplet, the second one would easily come to mind; similarly, if they could remember the rhyming words that ended each couplet, they could usually recall the lines in their entirety.

ESSENTIAL

Play some memory games with yourself as you did as a young child. Or, with a study buddy, come up with funny rhymes or mnemonic devices to help you remember facts.

Throughout history, many people have used short rhymes to help them remember various facts. Some of the more well-known rhymes used for mnemonic purposes are "In 1492, Columbus sailed the ocean blue" and "Thirty days hath September, April, June, and November." You can create your own rhymes to help you remember information about key terms for an exam. Try to find some word that rhymes with the term and write a short phrase or sentence that connects the two together. For example, if you want to remember what a mnemonic device is, you might remember this short rhyme: "Use a mnemonic device so you won't forget it twice."

Some terms lend themselves more easily to rhymes than others; if you can't come up with a rhyme relatively quickly, then try some other device so you won't waste much study time.

Alliteration

If there are two or more words together that begin with the same letter or sound, such as "King Kong" or "Peter Piper picked a peck of pickled peppers," you have alliteration. To use alliteration as a mnemonic device, take whatever key term you are trying to memorize and find some word beginning with the same sound that will trigger information about the term.

For example, the word "plethora," according to the dictionary, means "excess" or "abundance." You can associate "plethora" with "plenty." Since both plethora and plenty begin with the letter "P" (in fact, they both begin with the sound "pl"), it's much easier to remember the word "plenty" than "abundance." The word "plenty" makes you think of having too much of something; in other words, an abundance.

Mental Associations

Another mnemonic device is to think of a word or image you associate with both the term and its definition. This mental association functions as a link between the term and the information you hope to remember about it. For example, if you want to remember that Edison created the light bulb, you can look at Edison's name and see the word "son" in it. "Son" sounds just like "sun," so you can associate Edison's name with the sun. The sun, of course, is a source of light. So, by linking Edison with the sun, you can bring to mind the image of light and the light bulb.

Similarly, if you wanted to remember that Marconi invented the telegraph, you could stare at Marconi's name and see that it is similar to the word "macaroni." When you think of macaroni, you think of long strings of pasta. When you think of long strings, you think of telegraph wires. Therefore, you can link Marconi to telegraph wires with the image of macaroni.

When you try to create these mental associations, it's often helpful to rely on your personal experiences. For example, one student who needed to remember that John Keats wrote "Ode on a Grecian Urn" thought of her Uncle John who had visited Greece the previous summer. By linking "John" and "Greece" in her mind, she was able to remember that John Keats wrote the poem about the Grecian urn.

You can get as creative as you need to be in finding these associations. If necessary, you can think up a detailed, elaborate story that will help you link a word with information about it. And it can be as silly, illogical, or personal as you like, just so long as it works. A mental association only needs to make sense to you. You don't have to feel obliged to share it with other people.

Visualizations

You've probably heard the expression, "A picture is worth a thousand words." Well, it's also much easier to remember pictures than words. You can therefore use mental images and pictures instead of words and phrases to help you remember something. For example, one way to associate two or more words together is to create a picture in your mind that connects them.

If you want to remember that John Keats wrote "Ode on a Grecian Urn," for example, you might picture such an urn filled with enormous keys (which sounds like "Keats") inside of it.

Visualizations can be particularly helpful for associating several different terms or images together. If you want, for instance, to remember that the Department of Agriculture is part of the president's Cabinet, you can picture a stalk of corn inside of a large, oak cabinet. You can then add to that image by placing other objects in the cabinet to indicate other departments in the president's Cabinet, such as a giant penny to indicate the treasury, a gun to indicate the defense, and a set of scales to indicate justice.

Acronyms

An acronym is a word that is formed by taking the first letters from several words in a series such as SCUBA—S(elf) C(ontained) U(nderwater) B(reathing) A(pparatus). It can be instrumental in helping you remember a long list of items, especially if you need to remember them in a particular order.

For example, to remember the color spectrum, many students memorize the name "Roy G. Biv," an acronym made by taking the first letter of each color in the spectrum in order: R(ed), O(range), Y(ellow), G(reen), B(lue), I(ndigo), V(iolet).

ALERT

You can work on improving your vocabulary on your own. Almost any time you sit down to read, you'll probably encounter a new word (even in entertainment magazines or vacation beach reading bestsellers). Try to look up one new word that you've never heard before each time, and you will steadily build your vocabulary. You can use these new words in essays. Moreover, you will find that as your ability to read and interpret texts improves, so will your ability to read and interpret test questions.

Sometimes the first letters do not make a simple, easy-to-remember name like "Roy G. Biv." In those cases, you can create an entire sentence; the first letter of each word in the sentence corresponds to the first letter of the memorized terms. For example, in order to remember all of the planets in order, many students memorize this sentence: Mary's violet eyes make John stay up nights. The first letter of each word in that sentence corresponds to the first letter of a planet:

Mary's	Mercury
Violet	Venus
Eyes	Earth
Make	Mars
John	Jupiter
Stay	Saturn
Up	Uranus
Nights	Neptune

Yes, it's a silly sentence. But time and time again, it does the trick. And that's all that matters. Another commonly used acronym to learn the seven deadly sins is PEWGLAS: P(ride), (E)nvy, (W)rath, (G)luttony, (L)ust, (A)varice, (S)loth.

Repeated Exposure

The more times you expose yourself to material, the more ingrained it becomes in your long-term memory. To make certain you remember something, physically look at and think about it repeatedly over a long period of time. You are much better off studying a list of key terms for an hour each day, for five days, than studying it for five hours on one day. By looking at the list every day, you train yourself to retrieve that information from your memory after some time has passed. You'll find you get better at remembering information as the week passes; you'll begin to retrieve the information from your memory faster and with less effort. Learning becomes a habit.

Sleep on It

Believe it or not, studying right before you go to sleep can improve your memory recall of that information. Studies have shown that you are more likely to remember something you've read just before going to sleep. While you are asleep, your mind processes the information, moving it into your long-term memory. There's no guarantee that studying just before bed will be more effective than studying at other times, but it is certainly worth trying. Try reading over the master list of key terms right before you go to sleep; when you wake up the next morning, quiz yourself to see how much you remember. At the very least, studying the list each night for several nights before an exam ensures you expose yourself to the material repeatedly throughout your study period. And if in doubt, it cannot hurt to put your flash cards under your pillow and maybe through osmosis or luck their contents will seep through the pillow while you sleep!

Last-Minute Cram Cards

Sometimes, no matter how hard you study, you will find certain terms extremely difficult to memorize. When all other methods fail, you can create a last-minute cram sheet. The night before an exam, take a single index card and write down any terms, facts, phrases, or formulas you can't remember along with very brief definitions or explanations. Include especially any difficult terms likely to show up on an exam.

ALERT

Photocopy or scan the final version of your cram card and place an extra copy in a side pocket of your backpack or even your wallet. Often, students carry around this card right before a test and end up misplacing it. Having a backup just in case can be a lifesaver!

Take this card to the exam and arrive at the exam room a few minutes early so you can study the card before the examination begins. (You can sit at a desk in the exam room and study the card if this is allowed; otherwise, you can find a place to sit outside the room.) Continue to look at the card until you are asked to put away your notes. As soon as you receive your copy of the exam, before you look at a single question, write down everything you remember from the card in the margins of the examination booklet. Since you just looked at the card, the information on it should still be in your short-term memory, which means it should be easy for you to recall. You should be able to remember most of the information for at least five minutes.

The cram card is a particularly effective tool for math and science exams. You can write the formulas on the card and read them over right before the exam. At the start, you can then write the formulas somewhere in the exam book and refer back to them. You won't have to struggle to remember them every time you have to answer a question.

Studies have shown that reading frequently also improves writing ability. The more you read, the more comfortable you feel with language. As a result, you gain more of an instinct for what is written correctly; as you write, something will simply "sound right" or "sound wrong."

Getting Additional Help

If you need assistance in a class, first try to seek help directly from the teacher by going to his office hours or staying before or after class to ask questions. Do this especially in courses that are cumulative in nature (such as math) and the content of the course builds on a foundation of work done previously in the class. If you don't understand the basic fundamentals, then the homework, quizzes, and tests that build on each other can become too overwhelming for you and often result in a decline in your grades. Having your teacher on your side is a benefit. If she knows you are trying hard and seeking extra help from her, your effort will in some way be recognized in your grade at the end of the term. Also, remember: part of your grade earned on your report card is usually subjective. How well does your teacher know you and recognize the effort you put into her class? The relationship that you create with your teacher is important.

Professional tutors can be expensive, especially when you are paying for them (as opposed to your parents). See if you can find something to barter with your tutor if you cannot afford them. If you have a gift for building websites or can get them a discount at a store where you might work, see if a tutor will consider swapping services.

When working with your teacher is not possible or does not work for one reason or another, seek help in the form of a study group, study partner, or peer tutor. If you are in high school, don't be embarrassed or afraid to ask your parents or classmates to help you find a tutor in a subject that is particularly challenging for you. Many students—both honors and regular track—receive tutoring outside of class to reinforce and clarify what is being taught in class. Upperclassmen who have taken the course before you also can serve as great mentors or peer tutors. Also, many colleges and schools offer tutoring services through their academic support centers. You can be matched up with an upperclassmen or graduate student who can assist you in the subjects you need help in most.

ESSENTIAL

You might consider keeping a journal or blog either by hand or on your computer to improve your writing skills. Write down anything you wish in a journal—poetry, your thoughts and feelings, accounts of things you've done or accomplished, and descriptions of things you've seen or heard. You don't ever have to show the journal to anyone, so you don't have to worry about grammar or spelling. If you write in a journal frequently, you'll become more comfortable with writing in general, and more accustomed to setting your thoughts down on paper.

After you've tried those options, you could consider hiring a tutor. Hiring a tutor can help reinforce what you are learning in class and clarify work or reading assignments that you may have misunderstood or never understood before. The stigma of having a tutor (i.e., you must be dumb to not get what is going on) has waned through the years, and students often speak freely about the extra help they get from tutors. Tutors can also motivate you, help you with organization and study skills, and serve as an objective third party to your parents or teachers with regard to what is going on in class. A tutor can become a cheerleader and confidante as well. One-on-one attention can lead to great results. Just be sure you study together more than you socialize!

"Studying involves a ritual for me. I decompress before beginning by turning off my brain and watching some TV or surfing the Internet and eating a snack. Then I am all business. My study time is sacred and I take it very seriously. I remain focused, use a timer to keep me on task, and leave my cell phone in the other room turned off so I am not tempted to check a text or get distracted. My computer is only used for research or reference and not IM-ing or other distraction. My friends and roommate know to keep their distance when I am studying."

—Jocelyn R., Junior

CHAPTER 10

Preparing for Classroom Tests and Exams

Many students begin to panic before an exam because they've left themselves too much to worry about at the last minute. They find they still have to read assignments they never got to, reread assignments they don't remember, scrounge up notes for lectures they missed, and figure out what their disorganized lecture notes say. If you have been following the methods outlined in earlier chapters, you should already have clear, comprehensive notes from classroom lectures and reading assignments that include just about everything you need to know for an exam. Here's how to put it all together to study for a test.

Read Over All Your Notes

To begin studying for an upcoming exam, gather together all your notes from the course in one binder. This should not be a problem, since you've been putting your notes in a binder at home throughout the semester. Just make certain you now have them all in one place, in a logical order.

The first step is to read these notes from start to finish. It is extremely important that you do this in one sitting, *without interruption*. You'll need several hours to finish. This will help you concentrate more intently on the material; more important, it will enable you to develop a clear picture in your mind of the course material as a whole. Rather than studying various bits and pieces of information related to the subject, you'll now be able to see how everything fits together as part of the overall course.

Don't study several subjects at once, though, or one subject right after another. If you study several courses within a short period of time, the material can easily become mixed up in your mind, making it more difficult for you to remember specific details. Make certain you take a break of at least two hours before sitting down to read notes from another course.

Create Master Lists from Notes

As you read over your notes, condense and reorganize the material onto three single sheets of paper—the three master lists. You'll write one for key terms, one for key themes, and a third for related concepts. The preparation of these lists is itself a part of the study process; by reorganizing the material, you gain a firmer grasp on it. At the same time, the master lists serve as study tools; rather than having to read through all your notes again, you only need to study these three sheets. Each master list prepares you for a specific kind of examination question. The bulk of your preparation for the exam will center on working with these master lists.

The Master List of Key Terms

Create a master list of key terms from your notes by writing down any names, dates, concepts, or ideas that are central to the course; do not add any definition or explanation of them. Try to squeeze all the key terms on a single sheet of paper. Don't write down any of them more than once;

even if one comes up repeatedly throughout the course, you only need to write it down once. You may also decide to eliminate some key terms from the master list because you realize, in retrospect, that they aren't all that important.

The Master List of General Themes

Next, create a master list of general themes. As with the master list of key terms, try to squeeze all the general themes onto a single sheet of paper. If a particular theme recurs throughout the course, you don't need to write it down more than once; however, you should put a star beside it to indicate its importance.

The Master List of Related Concepts

Creating this particular master list is a bit more complicated and will likely take more thought and effort than the other two. It will prove helpful, however, in preparing for examination questions of all kinds.

As you read through your notes, try to identify groups of concepts that relate closely to one another. If you've identified such a group, write it down on the master list of related concepts and give it a subject heading.

A common category of related concepts is a principle or idea and the various examples that illustrate or support it. For example, you might be taking a history course in which the professor has argued repeatedly that the latter half of the Middle Ages was marked by increased pessimism and despair. You might then group together the various events your professor described that indicate this trend. For example:

REASONS FOR INCREASED PESSIMISM IN THE FOURTEENTH AND FIFTEENTH CENTURIES

- Weak kings (Edward II, Richard II) whose power was threatened by the barons
- One Hundred Years' War
- The Black Plague (1348)
- Skepticism in the church (after sale of pardons is sanctioned)

Here are other ways to group related concepts together that you might include on your master list:

- Events and causes (that lead up to them)
- Rules and exceptions
- Similar ideas, concepts, theories, and examples
- Opposite or dissimilar ideas, concepts, theories, and examples
- Chronologies/datelines
- Causes and effects

Try to identify and write down as many of these groups as you can. You may find yourself coming up with lots and lots of groups—that's all right for now. The process of reorganizing your notes this way encourages you to think, using the same kind of logic behind most examination questions.

You might have trouble, at first, fitting all the groups you identify on a single sheet of paper. If this is the case, use more than one sheet. As you work more with this master list, you can make decisions about what to eliminate and eventually condense the list onto a single sheet.

Working with the Master List of Key Terms

Becoming very familiar with key terms is a crucial part of preparing for an examination. For some terms, you will need to provide definitions; for others, you will need to know something about people, places, characters, or dates. For example, on a psychology exam, you might need to define the term "id." You might also need to know significant facts about Freud, such as that he conceived of the model of human personality consisting of the id, ego, and superego.

Many short-answer questions, such as multiple-choice, fill-in-the-blank, and true-or-false questions, are specifically designed to test your factual knowledge. The professor will be trying to see if you know the meaning of a particular term or the date of a certain event. You can't figure out the answer to these questions using reasoning or other kinds of skills—either you know the answer or you don't.

The following sample questions test factual knowledge of key terms.

1. An elegy is:
    A. a poetic inscription that ends with a witty turn of thought
    B. a fourteen-line poem written in iambic pentameter
    C. a formal poetic lament after the death of a particular person
    D. a long narrative poem documenting heroic actions

2. A fourteen-line poem written in iambic pentameter is:
    A. a sonnet
    B. an epigram
    C. an epic
    D. an elegy

3. A(n) _____ is a long narrative poem documenting heroic actions.

Key terms are also essential components of any essays you write for an exam. Your primary goal in answering an essay question is to demonstrate to the professor your knowledge and mastery of the subject matter. The more key terms you weave into an essay answer, the more you will impress the teacher with your knowledge and gain points on your essay.

As part of your exam preparation, therefore, you should spend a certain amount of time learning and testing yourself on key terms. After you have completed your master list, quiz yourself on the terms. Go down the list and try to define or say something significant about each term on the list.

If possible, quiz yourself in private and discuss each term out loud, as if you were explaining it to someone else in the room. This technique ensures that you explain each term fully. Many times, you look at a term, think you know it, and skip to the next one. You may not really be able to define the term as easily or as clearly as you think, though. By talking about each term, you see exactly how much you do or don't know about it. You also begin to feel more comfortable discussing these terms at length, which can help when you write an essay response.

Ultimately, you want to be able to go down the list and confidently define each term or say something about its significance. You probably won't be able to do that on the first shot. You might find yourself unable to remember a certain term or hesitating when you try to define or describe it in detail.

If that's the case, go back to your original notes and read more about the term. If many terms are giving you trouble, though, this can become a tedious and time-consuming process.

ESSENTIAL

The most important part of studying for a test is to use the system that works best for you. Whether it is using the ideas presented here or some other way you have found that works for you, find a system and implement it. Then learning and mastering material will become routine and a more structured process for you.

Instead of going back to your original notes, you can create a more detailed master list of key terms that includes brief definitions. Divide this master list into two columns, with the terms in the left column and the definitions in the right. The first few times you quiz yourself on the list, you can look at both columns; seeing the definitions will trigger your memory. After doing this a few times, cover the right column and see how you do when you quiz yourself only looking at the terms. If you get stuck on a term, simply look at the right column for the definition. Continue quizzing yourself this way until you no longer need to refer to the definitions at all.

Working with the Master List of General Themes

While preparing for an examination, the list of general themes can give you insight into what to study in detail; test questions almost always relate to the general themes rather than to more obscure points. You can therefore focus primarily on those key terms and concepts that relate to the general themes.

Your master list of general themes can also be a valuable tool in preparation for essay examinations. Short-answer questions are limited in scope; each short-answer question focuses on some specific piece of information. An essay question, though, requires elaboration. While answers to short-answer questions are often key terms or phrases, responses to essay questions must be several paragraphs long. And unlike short-answer questions that provide you with possible answers to choose from, the entire essay comes from a single source—you.

An essay question will therefore be relatively broad. It will not be on some obscure point because there would not be that much to write about. Instead, it will almost always refer to a major aspect of the course. In other words, an essay question almost always reflects one or more of the general themes.

Sometimes an essay question may be a simple reworking of a general theme. For example, if you are taking a course on Shakespeare, a general theme might be: "Shakespeare frequently experimented with the notion of genre; many of his plays defy classification into traditional genres." Possible essay questions that derive from that statement are:

- Discuss how Shakespeare experimented with the concept of genre.
- Choose three Shakespeare plays and discuss how they defy categorization into a specific genre.
- *Romeo and Juliet* is commonly considered an example of Shakespearean tragedy. There are a number of elements in it more common to comedy, however. Write an essay in which you discuss the comic aspects of *Romeo and Juliet.*

The first question essentially restates the general theme from the course into an essay topic. While the other questions are much more specific in terms of what they ask you to discuss, they still relate to the general theme involving the genre of Shakespeare's plays.

When you take an essay examination in class, you are pressed for time. That's why many responses are messy and unorganized. It's hard, after all, to come up with a detailed, focused response right on the spot. Luckily, you've been studying from your master list of general themes, which, as we've just seen, provides you with possible essay questions ahead of time. Examining the list and thinking about each theme, you can plan answers to the essay questions *before* the exam.

You don't have to write an elaborate practice essay for each theme or possible question you come up with, however. Instead, write down each general theme on a separate piece of paper. For each one, think about how you would approach an essay question related to that theme and make a list of the specific points, topics, and ideas you would incorporate into your response. If there are any key terms that also relate to the theme, list those as well.

Several times before the exam, sit down with these sheets and, using the list of points you've written for each theme, talk your way through the response you will write on the exam. By talking out loud, you will begin to feel more comfortable discussing these themes. Try to do this exercise at least twice for each theme—once looking at the detailed list of points and once looking at only the theme. If you can talk comfortably and at length about a general theme, you can write an essay about it on an exam.

Of course, there's no guarantee that essay questions on the exam will reflect these themes in their original form. Given that most essay questions address broad topics, however, they will usually connect in some way with a general theme. When you see the essay question, you can identify whichever theme it relates to, and draw on the same concepts you previously thought about in conjunction with that theme as you write.

Working with the Master List of Related Concepts

The answers to many short-answer questions are based on identifying a relationship between different ideas and terms. For example, many multiple-choice questions ask you to identify an example of some principle, theory, or idea:

Sample Question:
Which of the following is an example of a simile?
A. "O my love's like a red, red rose"
B. "Death, be not proud, though some have called thee"
C. "Beauty is truth, truth beauty"
D. "Shall I compare thee to a summer's day?"

Sometimes you might have to do the opposite, and identify the larger principle a particular example illustrates:

Sample Question:

"O my love's like a red, red rose" is an example of which type of figurative language?

A. personification
B. metaphor
C. simile
D. hyperbole

These questions can become more complicated when you need to identify several examples of a particular principle or theory and/or eliminate others that don't apply:

Sample Question:

I. "O my love's like a red, red rose"
II "Higher still and higher/From the earth thou springest/Like a cloud of fire"
III. "Beauty is truth, truth beauty"
IV. "Shall I compare thee to a summer's day?"

Which of the above is/are example(s) of a simile?

A. I and II only
B. III and IV only
C. all of the above
D. none of the above

For all these questions, you need to do more than define the key terms; you need to exercise a sense for which terms go together and why. That's where the master list of related concepts comes in. By having created this list, you've begun thinking with the same logic and in the same terms as the exam questions.

The master list of related concepts is also helpful in preparation for essay questions. In writing an essay, you may need to discuss a particular concept in detail. The master list helps identify the various topics and points that support a particular concept, providing detailed information you can include in your response. Moreover, by looking for the different groups of concepts and identifying how they are related, you have reconceptualized your notes.

Being able to rethink and reorganize different concepts indicates you have attained a certain degree of comfort and familiarity with these ideas.

The process of creating this master list involves a great deal of thought and effort. Once you've done it, which is the hard part, all you need to do is read it over a few times before the exam to keep the ideas fresh in your mind. Then you can enter an exam feeling confident about your ability to examine, think about, and answer complicated questions.

Make a Study Schedule

If you've been following all the strategies outlined in this book, then you've been studying all along. You still need to designate a certain amount of time prior to an exam to concentrate solely on studying for the exam using the strategies described in this particular chapter.

When planning your study schedule, you need to take into account the number of exams you are going to take and the amount of time you have available before each one. If you are preparing for only one exam and you have plenty of time to study, you can be flexible in your schedule. If you are studying for several exams in a brief time period, however, you need to create a strict schedule for yourself and devote certain hours each day to the study of specific subjects.

In general, you should avoid studying too long before the exam because you want the material you've studied to remain fresh in your mind. At the same time, you need enough time to go over your notes, to prepare and work with master lists of themes and topics, and to read additional sources and perhaps get extra help. To provide enough time to accomplish all this, you should begin studying about *five to seven days* before the examination.

Dividing Your Time into Stages

You can divide your study preparation into several stages.

1. The first stage, which you should do in one sitting, is to read through all your notes and create the master lists. Make certain you designate a large block of time (probably about four to six hours for each course) at the beginning of your study preparation period for this purpose.

2. The bulk of your study sessions should be devoted to working with the master lists, trying to memorize key terms, and talking your way through possible essay questions.
3. If you have the time, you can also read additional sources.

Divide your day into blocks of time devoted to different tasks; you might, for example, spend the morning reading sources in the library and the rest of the day working with your master lists.

Studying for Multiple Tests at Once

If you are studying for more than one examination, make certain to study only one subject at a time, and give yourself a break of at least one hour before beginning to work on another; otherwise the material can easily become mixed together in your mind. Create a study schedule that divides your day into different study sessions with breaks in between. Each study session should be devoted to preparing for a single examination.

Factor in Time for Your Well-Being

During the week prior to a major examination, it is extremely important that you get plenty of sleep and eat well. Your mind is doing some hard work, so let your body take a rest sometimes. You may feel you are getting a great deal accomplished by staying up late, but you are actually doing more harm than good. When you get overly tired, it becomes much more difficult to retrieve information from your long-term memory. If you arrive at an examination feeling exhausted, you won't be able to work through problems with a clear head.

The night before a major exam, you should give yourself a break and take it easy. That doesn't mean you should take the *whole* night off, though. Read over your study materials one final time to keep all of the information fresh in your mind, then watch TV or go to a movie. And make certain you get a good night's sleep.

A Step-by-Step Plan

Here are some lists to help you map out a plan for preparing for exams.

BEFORE YOU BEGIN STUDYING (BEFORE CLASSES END)

- Get information from the professor on exam content and format.
- Try to get sample tests if available.
- Find out date, time, and location of the exam.
- Consider joining a study group with other hardworking and intelligent students.

FIVE TO SEVEN DAYS PRIOR TO EXAM

- Read through all notes from classroom lectures and reading assignments.
- Create the three master lists (key terms, general themes, and related concepts). Take four to six hours per subject to do this.

TWO TO FIVE DAYS PRIOR TO EXAM

- Quiz yourself on each master list for each subject every day.
- Work with cue cards and use other memorization techniques to learn key terms.
- Take notes on general themes and talk your way through possible essays.
- See the professor to ask last-minute questions, if you have any.
- Meet with study group or partners, if you opt to do this.
- Read other sources, if time allows.
- Make certain you know where to go for the exam. Confirm the day, time, and location. If you are unfamiliar with the test site, go there before the test day so you can see exactly where it is and how much time it takes to get there.

THE NIGHT BEFORE THE EXAM

- Conduct one final read-through of the master lists.
- Talk your way through possible essays.
- Make a cram sheet of terms you still can't retain.
- Relax: See a movie or watch TV.
- Gather items to bring to the exam: pens (that work), watch (that works), candy, gum, a drink, your final cram sheet, and other materials you may need (such as a calculator, books, etc.).
- Get a good night's sleep.
- Set two alarms before going to sleep!

THE DAY OF THE EXAM

- Talk about some key terms and general themes in the shower for a mental warm-up.
- Eat a balanced meal with some protein the day of the test. Too many carbohydrates the day of might feel like good comfort food, but if you eat too much right before the test, carbs turn to sugars and then you might peak and then "crash" and be less alert during the test. Instead, opt for your comfort food the day *before* the exam.
- Stay hydrated, too, but not so hydrated that you have to leave the test to use the bathroom constantly!
- If you have an afternoon or evening exam, use the morning for a final read-through of your master lists.
- Make certain you bring writing implements and a watch to the exam.
- Get to the exam site early to choose a good seat.

QUOTE

"If I plan ahead and take the time to make master lists, then studying for tests and finals is a breeze. I have made my own little personalized version of 'Spark/Cliffs Notes' which is manageable and easy to digest and review come study time."

—Marcia B., Sophomore

CHAPTER 11

Tests and Exam Preparation Tips

When it comes to preparing for tests there are a variety of approaches you can take and tactics to consider. It may take some trial and error for you to see which approaches work for you based on your comfort level with the subject, the type of test you are taking (in-class essay, multiple choice, final paper, etc.), or even the environment in which you take the exam.

Working with Study Partners or Study Groups

In preparing for tests and exams, you might decide to form a study group or work with a partner. This format for studying is not for everyone, however. Before deciding whether or not a study group would help you, consider these advantages and disadvantages.

Advantages of a Study Group

When you get together with other students, you have the opportunity to learn from one another. One classmate, for example, may have better notes or a better grasp of a particular subject than you do. You can use him or her as a source of information to flesh out certain points in your own notes. Answering questions from your fellow students will also help you study. Talking about a particular topic is an excellent way to gain familiarity with the material. In the process of describing and explaining a concept to someone else, you develop a better understanding of it yourself.

Being part of a study group also ensures that you study a certain amount of time before an exam; the group keeps you on a set study schedule. If you have difficulty motivating yourself to study, being part of a study group can give you the jump-start and structure you need.

Perhaps most important, being part of a study group provides emotional support during a difficult time. Studying for and taking exams is an extremely stressful, emotionally draining experience, especially if you feel alone. Meeting regularly with friends going through the same experience can make you feel better. These meetings alleviate tension as you laugh with your friends and help one another through the rough spots.

Disadvantages of Study Groups

If the students in your study group have poor notes and don't really understand the subject matter themselves, you might spend all your time helping them and not receive any help in return. You need to watch out for "moochers" who haven't done any work all year and merely want to copy your notes. Panicky students are also a serious problem in a study group. There may be members who are so stressed out that, instead of providing emotional support, they make you more nervous about an exam than you were before. Additionally, the bulk of the study group's time may be spent trying to calm this one person down or discussing only those concepts he doesn't understand.

Study groups often don't use time efficiently. You may spend several hours with a study group and find you've only covered a small portion of the material, much less than you could have on your own. There are several reasons why this might occur. Whenever a group of students get together, there is going to be a certain amount of chatting, joking, and socializing. Another problem is that a large portion of time might be spent discussing some point you already understand; that's obviously not the best use of your time.

ALERT

If you find your study group or partner is becoming more of a social group or a distraction for you from your studies, find another group or study alone. While your intentions may be good in partnering with others, sometimes getting out of a group that is really not helping you to improve as a student is a better choice to make.

Choosing the right people to work with is the way to avoid some of these major disadvantages. A good study group involves give and take among all members; everyone should be willing to work and should have something valuable to contribute to the group. It's also a good idea to limit the size of the group; any more than five members will probably waste more time and be more trouble than it's worth.

At the same time, if you think that you work better on your own, don't feel you are at a disadvantage. Being in a study group is no guarantee of study success.

Review Sessions

Professors occasionally organize formal review sessions prior to an examination, where they or a teaching assistant are available to answer questions regarding course material. You should attend these study sessions even if you don't have a specific question. You never know what hints a professor might share about what will be on the test. It's also helpful to hear the professor or T.A. describe again the major concepts and key terms. Try to use some of their phrases and terminology on your exam responses.

ESSENTIAL

Try to prepare thoughtful questions for your review session. Be an active listener and seek clues in what your professor or T.A. presents that may help indicate what will be on an upcoming exam.

Be cautioned, though, that these sessions tend to attract panicky students who use the time to voice their own fears and anxieties about the exam. In addition to wasting time in the session, these students can also make you feel stressed out. Do your best to ignore them. The only person you need to listen to at the review session is the professor or teaching assistant. Another problem that might arise is that one or two students will dominate the entire session with their questions. If you have a question, ask it right at the beginning to guarantee a response.

Read and Review Other Sources

Consulting with and reading additional sources is a valuable study technique in the days prior to an examination. Your priority, however, is creating and working with the three master lists. Only if you have additional time during your study preparation period, should you read other sources, particularly when you have trouble understanding something from a lecture or reading assignment. As you go over your notes and prepare the master lists, you may come across terms or ideas that you still don't understand. You also may find that, as time passes, you forget important information. If so, turn to reliable online sources, test prep books by subject available at your local bookstore, or go to the library for more information.

Many academic encyclopedias and dictionaries, for example, might include listings for the key terms you've studied in class. By consulting these sources, you can find clear and concise explanations of these points. Use your computer to look up sources or seek the assistance of a librarian at your school or local library.

Even if you are not confused about a particular point, it's a good idea to read some additional sources anyway. The more sources you read, the more information you receive. And by reading about a subject in depth just before an exam, you immerse yourself in the material; you then enter the examination focused on, and comfortable with, that subject.

FACT

Study aides such as CliffsNotes or SparkNotes can be great tools if used properly. Be sure to use them as a supplement, not to replace reading a primary source. Consult them when the original text confuses you or you think you missed a significant theme or concept.

Consulting introductions to different editions of important primary texts can provide additional information. For example, an introduction to a particular work of literature will often summarize the plot, describe the characters, and discuss major thematic and critical issues. Reading these introductions helps you recall the work in more detail, while providing ideas you might not have considered. You can also look for anthologies and collections that include articles and essays on a particular subject or by a certain writer. For example, an introduction to a volume of *Freud's Collected Writings* might summarize his major innovations, as well as the controversies surrounding them.

Reading about the same topic in several sources is a worthwhile exercise because it shows how the subject can be described in different ways. This is important, as examination questions will often be worded in a manner different from the way the material was originally described to you.

ALERT

Teachers and professors are familiar with study aides sold in stores (such as CliffsNotes, SparkNotes, or lecture notes) and often avoid testing on areas that these study aids cover in great length. Be sure you are familiar with your text as a whole and not just the highlights reviewed in a study supplement.

Other sources can also provide a variety of examples and illustrations of major principles. Finding additional examples can be particularly helpful in preparing for math and science examinations for which you are asked to complete various problems using different formulas. Seeing a variety of sample problems before an exam makes you better prepared to answer problems yourself; you are able to see the many different problems that relate to a particular formula or principle. You can even find sources with sample problems and solutions, so that you can practice with actual questions.

Here are some ideas for additional sources:

- Academic encyclopedias and dictionaries. You can consult general ones such as the *Encyclopedia Americana* or *Encyclopaedia Britannica*, or ones for specific subjects, such as arts and humanities, world and U.S. history, or science and technology. Ask the reference librarian for suggestions or seek online versions of these or similar sources.
- Introductions to various editions of a particular text, such as a work of literature, or to collections and anthologies of works on specific subjects or by specific writers.
- Additional textbooks on the same subject (check the index and table of contents to quickly find sections you want to read).
- Additional books or articles on the same subject. For suggestions, check the bibliography or list of works cited in your textbook or the section of the library or bookstore where books on that subject are shelved.
- Study guides on different subjects specifically written for high school or college students. Just be certain you only use these guides to supplement your own notes, not to take the place of them.

Talk to the Professor

The most obvious source for information about an exam is the professor; after all, the professor is the one who makes up the questions. Most professors take a few minutes during a class to explain the format and the material to be covered. If an exam is approaching and the professor has not made such an announcement, you can take the initiative and ask.

Although you can inquire in class, talking to the professor after class or during office hours is, in some ways, more effective. The professor will be more inclined to talk with you at length when it's not taking up other students' time. You'll be able to ask more questions and, if you're lucky, the professor might offer you more detailed information about the exam than he would in class.

These are some basic questions you can ask a professor about an upcoming exam:

- What will be the format of the exam? Will there be short-answer questions? What type? Multiple-choice questions? Will there be essays? A combination of types of questions?
- How many sections will there be on the exam? How many points will each section be worth?
- What percentage of your overall grade is determined by the exam?
- What material from class will be covered on the exam?
- If the exam is a final, will the exam be cumulative (meaning it covers the entire semester's worth of material)? Or will it only cover a portion of the course material since the midterm or midyear?
- Do you have any suggestions on how to study for the exam?

Try to see the professor at least one week before a scheduled exam; that gives you enough time to plan your study schedule accordingly.

Find Exams on the Same (or Similar) Courses

You can often get a highly accurate sense of what an upcoming exam will be like by looking at previous exams. In addition to providing examples of the kinds of questions likely to be included, these can be used for practice runs to test yourself on the course material.

Some departments keep exams on file so that students may use them as a study resource. You can also try to find someone who has already taken the course and held onto the exams and who is willing to lend them to you. Just make certain that you are not doing anything unethical in looking at old examinations. If the professor has given a graded exam back to the students, then she knows it is available for anyone to examine. On the other hand, if the professor collects the exams and does not return them, then she doesn't intend for them to be distributed among students.

If you somehow get a pirated copy of an exam, you are committing a serious breach of ethics that can get you in big trouble. When you consider the penalties, you'll realize that it's just not worth the risk.

ESSENTIAL

Try to find an old exam from the same course you are taking that was made up by your professor. This provides you with the most accurate picture of the exam you can expect to take.

Listen for Clues

Throughout the semester, keep your ears open for any clues about what might be on an exam. Clues can crop up anytime, so be on the lookout. A professor might say, in a completely casual manner, that a particular concept or term is likely to show up on the exam. After making a certain point, a teacher might say something like, "If I were to ask a question on an exam about this topic, I'd ask you . . ." Anytime your professor makes any reference to an exam, even in an offhand manner, make certain you note and "star" it.

In addition to blatant clues, the professor will probably give you subtle ones. Exam questions always reflect the professor's personal interests and biases. Even if the course is a basic survey course, there are certain to be some topics your teacher feels are more important for you to know and are therefore more likely to show up on an exam. Anything your professor seems particularly serious or passionate about is a likely candidate for inclusion. Any point your professor makes repeatedly, or gives special attention to, is also more likely to appear on an exam. Star these points in your notes to remind yourself to study them before an exam.

If You Do Cram

The most effective way to study for an exam is to take several days, ideally a week, in which to prepare. Of course, not everyone is able to do that all the time. If you do find yourself having to cram the day or night before a major test, do it wisely. The worst thing you can do is to pull an "all-nighter," drinking loads of caffeine or Red Bull to keep you awake. Even if you cover a great deal of material in those hours, you'll be so exhausted the next day you won't have the stamina to make it through the exam. You may know the material, but you won't have the energy to write a detailed essay, and your mind will be so foggy that you won't be able to remember what you did study. You can cram, but make certain you get enough hours of sleep to function and be alert.

If you haven't taken detailed notes from classroom lectures and reading assignments all semester, then you have a problem. It is extremely difficult at the last minute to catch up on all that material. If you've gotten yourself into this situation, then you should probably gamble and read only certain assignments carefully. If there's time, try to skim as many readings as possible. In order to skim a text, read some or all of the following elements:

- Introductions and conclusions
- Summary paragraphs
- Chapter title and subtitles
- Any words or phrases that are bold, italicized, or underlined (If the terms are unfamiliar to you, read the entire sentence.)
- Captions for diagrams and photographs
- First and last lines of all paragraphs

As you skim, if a particular word, phrase, or line catches your attention and seems significant, consider reading the entire paragraph.

Cramming and rushing through readings are not ideal ways to feel ready for any academic challenge. In fact, once you have been through the experience of cramming and skimming texts, you may find the anxiety you experience while trying to catch up on a semester or entire school year is just too stressful and not worth it. Remember how this feels the next time testing rolls around and maybe you will find yourself wanting to be better prepared.

Finishing Your Marathon

You may think that passing an exam is solely a matter of how much of the course material you've memorized. An exam is just as much a test of mental and physical endurance as it is your knowledge of a particular subject, however. In that sense, it's somewhat akin to running a marathon. Even though most marathon runners run almost every day, they move their training into high gear during the weeks before a major race, running longer hours and farther distances so they will be ready for the upcoming event. Most high-level athletes work hardest during the final minutes of a game, pushing themselves to hustle and finish strong.

You, too, should move your studying into high gear before a test, focusing your energy more on the subject matter. The methods and strategies previously outlined will help you do that. You don't need to be a bookworm or genius to ace a test, but you do need to be an academic athlete, willing to train hard with the goal of achieving a winning grade on an upcoming exam.

Dealing with Panic

Regardless of how prepared or ill prepared you may be, preparing for and taking examinations is stressful. When stress becomes panic, it is a serious problem that plagues many students. Before an exam, panic can keep you from studying effectively; in the midst of an exam, it can mean the difference between success and failure. Here are some helpful strategies for fighting panic.

Have a Plan of Attack

One important antidote to panic is having a clear, well-thought-out plan of attack. Not having a plan is like going on a trip without a map—you worry about where you're going and, before you know it, you're lost. Having a strategy to fall back on puts you more in control of the situation and more confident of your abilities.

Remember the Big Picture

One major cause of panic is the tendency to blow the significance of exams completely out of proportion, to think of each exam as a matter of life or death. It's extremely important to put the experience into perspective by remembering the big picture. A single examination is only a small part of your overall educational experience and an even more minuscule part of your life. In future years, no one is ever going to ask how you did on a specific exam in school. You probably won't even remember the exam yourself.

ESSENTIAL

Bombing a test will not scar you forever. Learn from your mistakes and do better next time. Try to determine everything you did wrong so you can move forward and recover from your setback.

Moreover, doing poorly on an examination is not a reflection of you as a person. It's not even an indication of intelligence. Some people are simply better at taking exams than others because they've developed successful test-taking skills—skills that you can also learn. Doing poorly on one exam does not mean you'll do poorly on others. If you find you continue to do badly, you should seek help. Most colleges, for example, offer special tutoring services. You can work regularly with a tutor and, most likely, improve your examination performance.

Avoid Alarmists

At all costs, stay away from the alarmists. These are other students who, completely stressed out themselves, try to pass their panic on to you. What is truly alarming is how successful they can be at shaking your own confidence. Once they approach you and convey their own fears, you'll find you, too, are starting to get nervous. Panic is infectious; before you know it, you'll be freaking out right alongside them.

Be especially wary of rumors. Chances are what you hear about the level of difficulty of an upcoming examination or about specific questions are just rumors. If you let them sidetrack you from your own study preparations, you'll be wasting time. Avoid alarmists as much as possible, especially in the days before an exam. If an alarmist corners you and asks how you feel about the exam, politely tell her you are studying as best you can and don't want to worry about what is on the exam until you get there.

Avoid talking to alarmists right before an examination begins. Many will get to the examination room early and ask fellow students to explain things they don't understand. There's really no point explaining various terms; this only gets everyone into a nervous frenzy just as the examination is being passed out. Don't talk about the test or the material with other people. The last thing you need to worry about before an exam begins is how much someone else understands. Stay calm and focus your thoughts and be confident about what you've already studied.

ALERT

Don't let panicked classmates freak you out. If you have studied and know the material you are being tested on, try to block out others' panic and think for yourself. You can succeed despite their dire predictions! Don't let the fears of others bring you down.

Take Breathers

Studying for and taking examinations is a physically and mentally exhausting procedure. It's crucial that you give yourself frequent breaks to help you relax. Don't study for more than two hours without taking a breather. Take a short walk, stretch your muscles. Even a ten- or fifteen-minute break can help you feel revived.

It's just as important that you take a breather while taking an examination. If you are not worried about the time, you can take a short break in the middle of the exam by asking to be excused to get a drink or go to the bathroom. If you don't want to leave the room, you can take a breather right at your seat. Put your pen down and give your hands a short rest. Take your eyes off the exam booklet and look out the window or around the room; just make certain you don't look anywhere near another person's paper, or you might be accused of cheating. Lift your arms in the air to stretch your back muscles and roll your head around to ease tension in your neck. Take several really deep breaths. A breather like this only needs to take about thirty seconds, but it will help you remain calm and focused during the exam.

Practice Relaxation Exercises

There are many relaxation techniques that psychologists and therapists teach for coping with stress and panic. You can use these techniques while studying for exams and even while taking them. If you are particularly prone to stress, you may want to buy a book or audio guide that teaches relaxation exercises and practice them all semester.

Visualization Exercise

Here is one basic technique that you can start doing right away. You should try to do this exercise a few times before an exam so that it will work more effectively during an actual test.

As you practice this exercise, you'll be able to experience that feeling of safety and happiness more and more quickly—in as little as thirty seconds—just by closing your eyes and breathing deeply. Even during an exam, you can take thirty seconds to close your eyes, breathe deeply, and relax.

Sit in a chair with a firm back and place your palms, face up, on your thighs. Close your eyes, and take deep breaths. Concentrate for a few moments only on your breathing, on the feeling of air going into and out of your lungs. Next, picture yourself someplace you've been where you felt safe and happy. See yourself there. Use all your senses. Remember the sights, smells, and sounds of being there. Think about this scene for several moments, continuing to breathe deeply. Enjoy the feeling of safety and serenity you know while you are there. At the same time, know that you can always return there, where you feel safe and happy, when you need to. Sit for as long as you like in this place. When you are ready to leave, count to ten, and then open your eyes.

Other Relaxing Activities

Try other ways to relax. Attend a yoga, stretching, or other relaxing exercise class offered at your school or local community center. Just following a trainer's instructions can assist you in centering yourself, refocusing, and calming your anxiety.

Or, play music you enjoy in a quiet place like your bedroom or even in the privacy of your car. Focus on the different elements of the music, heightening your senses to the sounds that you hear. Focus on the music and also your breathing. Allow the song to soothe you. Or, you could get a sound machine for your room or download other songs that offer white noise, the sounds of nature, or running water. Keep these soothing sounds on to help you get calm.

"Through the years I have found that participating in study groups can be either the best or the worst experience. For me, being in a study group for a subject that does not come easily to me serves as a terrific supplement to class lectures, notes, and assignments. Conversely, I am not sure how much value I add as a member of that group, so I also try to participate in a study group for a subject that I master so that I can lead and share what I know."

—Michele M., Junior

CHAPTER 12

Taking Tests and Exams

The hour or two that you sit for your exam demonstrates to the teacher what you have learned, how you analyze and grasp the content of the class, and even how well your teacher has taught the material. In many cases, your entire grade comes down to this one test. Don't forget to breathe deeply and feel confident that you have done your best to prepare.

The Morning of Exam Day

The most crucial thing to remember on the day of the exam is to set your alarm and give yourself enough time to get ready, especially if your exam is in the morning. More than one student has slept through a major exam, and it's hard to get sympathy from the professor when this happens. If your alarm is unreliable, or if you have the habit of turning it off in your sleep or hitting the snooze button, then set several alarms including your cell phone, laptop, or watch. You may even want to arrange to have a friend or relative give you a back-up wake-up call.

ESSENTIAL

Get enough sleep TWO nights before your exam. Sometimes a lack of sleep from a previous night doesn't hit you the next morning but lags a day. So, get your rest leading up to your test and eat healthy!

When you take a shower that morning, try talking to yourself about some of the key terms or general themes you've prepared on the master list. This mental exercise serves to get your brain warmed up and focused on the subject matter. (If you feel comfortable enough, you could even talk out loud.) If your exam is in the afternoon or evening, you can read over your master lists in the morning. But don't overburden yourself. A final read-through should be all you need to put you in the right frame of mind for the exam. Don't spend this time trying to memorize or learn new material. After this read-through, do something to take your mind off the exam, such as taking a walk or watching TV.

On the day of the test, eat a well-balanced meal with some protein to give your body an energy boost. Don't eat too large a meal, though—that will make you sleepy.

Make certain you know exactly where the exam is being given and leave yourself enough time to get there. Try to get to an exam about fifteen minutes before it is scheduled to start; this will ensure you don't arrive late, flustered, and out of breath. You also want to have the benefit of the entire allotted time, from the first minute to the last.

Bring several pens of blue or black ink, or pencils and a sharpener if it is a standardized test, and a good watch. You might also want to bring some gum, candy, or a water bottle, if it is allowed. Make certain your watch is working or that there is a clock in the room: It is crucial to keep track of time during the exam.

ALERT

When you get to the exam, choose your seat carefully. You might, for example, want to sit near a window so that you can look up every so often and take a break. You also want to sit where you can see the clock.

Before the exam begins, avoid talking about anything related to the test with other students, especially alarmists and panickers. You can sit at your desk and glance over your master lists or a last-minute cram sheet if you've made it. But don't get involved in a detailed question-and-answer session with other students; it's really too late to learn any major point. Moreover, if you listen to someone else, you risk becoming confused about a point you were previously quite certain that you understood. This will only serve to make you more anxious. Stay calm so that you can take the exam with a clear head.

Test-Taking Strategies

When you arrive at the testing classroom or exam site you should try to have your mindset clear and remain as relaxed as possible. At this point you either know it or you don't, so just hope that your preparation was sufficient and there will not be too many surprises awaiting you.

When you get the exam, don't just dive in and begin answering questions. Instead, take a moment to glance through the entire exam to see how it is structured and get a sense of the kinds of questions waiting for you. That way you can devise a plan of attack that ensures you use your time most efficiently. This preliminary read-through minimizes the tendency to panic midway through the exam.

Look through the exam to see how many sections there are, the type of questions included, and the point values for each section. Then create a rough mental schedule for yourself allotting a certain amount of time for each section, depending on how many points it is worth and the level of difficulty.

Obviously, the more points a section is worth, the more time you should devote to it. For example, if an hour-long exam is divided into a short-answer section worth fifty points and an essay portion worth fifty points, then you should spend an equal amount of time for each section, thirty minutes. If the short-answer section is worth only thirty points, however, and the essay portion is worth seventy, then you should spend much more time on the essay section. But you should also take into account the levels of difficulty of each section. For example, if you find short-answer questions much easier than essays, you can allot additional time to the essay portion of the exam by getting the short answers done and out of the way.

The other advantage to looking at the entire exam beforehand is that you won't have any surprises waiting for you. It is extremely helpful, for example, to know if there is an essay section following the multiple-choice questions. That way, while you are answering the multiple-choice questions, you can also be thinking about how you will approach the essay. You might also come across short-answer questions that include terms or give you ideas for things to include in the essay.

Strategies for Short-Answer Questions

There are three types of short-answer questions that are commonly asked on examinations: fill-in-the-blank, true-or-false, and multiple-choice. Although there are different strategies for each type of question, you can follow the same techniques.

Read the Directions

Students often make the mistake of diving right into the questions without reading the directions. The directions include important information you need to know *before* you start answering questions. You may, for example, not be expected to answer all questions on the exam but have a choice.

You won't know that, though, unless you read the instructions. It would be unfortunate to take the time to answer all fifty multiple-choice questions, when the directions told you to choose only thirty. Or you may be asked to select three of the following five short essay questions to answer. The directions might also indicate whether you are penalized for incorrect answers. If you are penalized, then you won't want to guess as often. In general, get all the facts about the examination before beginning.

Read Each Question Carefully

With all short-answer questions, it is extremely important that you read the question carefully. Read the entire question and, if it is a multiple-choice question, all the possible choices as well. Don't read the first few words or skim the question and think you know the answer. Sometimes the wording of a question (or the choices on a multiple-choice question) will look familiar, and you'll therefore assume you know the answer; but when you read the question carefully, you may find that even if an answer sounds right, it's still not.

When students get short-answer questions wrong, it's often the fault of "trick words" they've overlooked. These are crucial words tucked into the question that completely determine the correct answer but are easily not caught. Here is a list of trick words frequently tucked into exam questions: *not, always, sometimes, never, all, some, none, except, more,* and *less.*

Always be on the lookout for these "trick words"; if you see one, underline it in the question so you can keep it in mind as you attempt to determine the answer. And never assume, just because a true-or-false statement or a possible choice in a multiple-choice question looks familiar, that it is necessarily true or correct. There could be one word tucked in the sentence that invalidates the entire statement.

Pace Yourself

Time is of the essence, especially on an exam. You've therefore got to watch the clock and pace yourself to make certain you get to all the questions.

When you first get the exam, look at the total number of questions and how much time you have to answer them. You can then figure out approximately how much time you have to answer each one; of course, you may spend more time on the harder questions and less time on the easy ones, but it should average out. Check the time frequently. It's a good idea to get in the habit of checking your watch every time you turn the page of the exam. Monitor your progress and look at how many more questions you have to go. If you find you are going too slowly, then try to pick up the pace.

ESSENTIAL

In multiple-choice tests, if you choose to skip a question, circle the number of the question you skipped on both your tests AND answer sheet so that you remember to go back. Otherwise you will be off by a number, which can foul up your entire test.

Difficult questions will require more thought and time. When you get stuck on a particular question, you risk using up time that could be spent answering easier questions—the ones you immediately know the answers to, without a doubt. If you come across a very difficult question, skip it for the moment; that way you make certain you will get to all the questions you can answer easily and earn all of those points. Circle the difficult questions so you can find them when you go back. After completing all of the easy questions, go back to the tricky questions and take the remaining time to work on them.

Intelligent Guessing

Chances are, you are not going to know the answer to every single question on an examination; on a short-answer question, though, you can always guess. And if you guess intelligently, you have a decent shot at getting it right. Intelligent guessing means taking advantage of what you *do* know in order to try to figure out what you *don't*. It makes much more sense than random guessing.

Guessing on Fill-in-the-Blank Questions

These are the most difficult to make guesses on because you usually need to furnish the answer independently; you aren't always given a selection of choices as you are on a multiple-choice question. Try to identify a general theme that the question reflects, and think about the key terms that relate to it. There's a strong chance that one of those terms will be the correct answer. You can also look for and underline the key terms within the statement and think about any related concepts you have learned in class.

Guessing on True-or-False Questions

It almost always pays to guess on these because you have a fifty-fifty chance of getting it right. If you are uncertain about the answer, test the statement by finding specific cases that support or counter it. For example, if the statement asserts that a particular phenomenon is always true, you only need to think of a single case when that statement is not true and the answer will be false. Similarly, if the word "never" is included, you only need to think of a single case when the statement is true, and it will be false. When you come up with specific cases that support your guess, you can be confident that your answer is correct.

Guessing on Multiple-Choice Questions

The key to guessing on these is to eliminate as many of the choices as you can. With each elimination, you raise the odds of picking a correct response. If you can narrow down to two choices, then you've got a fifty-fifty chance of getting it right—the same odds as on a true-or-false question.

There will usually be at least one choice you can eliminate right off the bat because it is obviously wrong. After that, examine each choice and see if there is anything incorrect within the answer itself. If the choice can't stand on its own as an accurate statement, then it is probably not a correct answer and you can eliminate it. For example, a possible choice might include a key term with the wrong definition. In that case, you know it won't be the right response. Finally, you can eliminate choices that don't reflect the same general theme as the question. A choice that relates to a completely different theme most likely will not be the correct answer.

Many multiple-choice questions include the options "all of the above" and "none of the above." When these statements are included, it becomes much easier to make a guess. Look at the other choices. If you identify one that you think is an accurate answer, you can confidently eliminate the "none of the above" option. By the same token, if you are only allowed to include one answer, and you find two choices that are accurate answers, the "all of the above" option must be the correct answer.

ALERT

Watch out for choices that, on their own, are correct and accurate statements; they aren't always the correct answer to the question. Just because a choice is itself an accurate statement doesn't mean it is correct in the context of the question.

Once you narrow down the responses to two options, don't spend too much time pondering and evaluating which one is the right choice. Just go with your gut instinct; your first impressions are usually right. And once you've put in your guess, don't go back and change it unless you later figure out the correct response with absolute certainty. Sometimes, for example, a later question will include information that sparks your memory or helps you figure out the answer to an earlier question. If that happens, go back and change the answer. Otherwise, forget about the question and forge ahead.

Visualizations

You might find, in the midst of an exam, that you've forgotten some piece of information you are certain that you studied. This can be particularly frustrating because the answer is stuck somewhere in your long-term memory and you are having trouble accessing it. Close your eyes and try to picture the page from your notes or the master list on which the information is included. Try to "see" the page in your mind. Can you "read" the information on the page? Picture yourself studying those notes wherever you actually studied. Sometimes by seeing where you originally studied some piece of information, you can remember it. If none of that works, skip the question and move on to others. You may find that, as you answer other questions, you will remember the information you needed for an earlier one. Memory is a mysterious mechanism; sometimes it resists pressure until you are distracted.

A Word on Penalties

On some examinations, you are penalized more for putting in an incorrect answer than for leaving the question blank. On those tests, it won't pay to guess as often. If you can narrow down your choices to two or even three possibilities, however, it is usually to your advantage to guess, since the odds are in your favor.

If You Have Trouble Understanding the Question

Read over a difficult question a few times to see if you can at least get the gist of it. Don't worry about specific words you don't know. Focus, instead, on what the question is essentially asking. Does it want you to furnish a key term? Provide a definition of a term? Provide an example or illustration of some idea? Figure out the exception to some rule? If you can grasp the nature of the question, you may be able to narrow down the possible answers.

QUESTION

What if I do not understand a test question?
If there is a question that you just plain do not understand, go to the professor, teacher, or proctor and ask. Chances are some other classmates had similar questions and if enough of you ask, perhaps clarification will be addressed or announced during the test time. If you never ask, you risk being penalized and not being able to make up for the error.

When you read over the question, underline any key terms. What general theme or topic is associated with those key terms? If you think more about that general theme, what related concepts or issues come to mind? Do any of these topics seem to tie into the question? If it is a multiple-choice question, look at the various choices. Do you understand them? Do any of them contain key terms that are familiar? Sometimes, even if you don't understand a specific question, you may be able to make a guess based on your overall knowledge of its general theme.

Writing Essays for Tests

Since you've brainstormed possible essay topics as you reviewed your master lists, you will likely find that you are prepared for at least most of the essay questions on your exam. You can recall how you "talked through" possible essays and write some responses using that framework. Here are some additional tips.

Read the Questions Carefully

Don't begin writing until you have read the questions in their entirety and are certain you understand them. Essay questions will not always be written in a straightforward manner and you may have to think about what exactly is being asked of you. Sometimes, for example, teachers write lengthy essay questions that include more information than the actual question, such as quotations or anecdotes. Or there may be several questions related to a common topic, all of which you are expected to address in your response. There are also essay questions that are not even phrased as questions, but tell you to "discuss" or "address" some topic. Read carefully and try to identify exactly what you need to cover in your essay. Underline any lines or phrases that specifically indicate points you are to consider.

If You Must Make a Choice

On many exams, rather than being given a single essay question, you will be given a choice of questions. Choose carefully, and select the question you can write the most impressive essay on. For each one, consider your knowledge of the topic and the specific points you would present in an essay. You might even jot down a few notes next to each question, indicating your thoughts. Choose the question you have the most to say about and feel most confident answering. Don't waste much time agonizing over the choices—that's time that could be spent actually writing. Look at the questions, think about each one, make your decision, and go with it.

Once you've made your decision, stick with it. Students sometimes lose their nerve halfway through their essay and decide to try answering a different question. But by then they have little time left, making it difficult, if not impossible, to write an adequate response. You are generally better off sticking with your first choice and doing the best you can; even if you get stuck midway, you've probably written more than you could if you started on another.

If the Question Is Confusing or Difficult

It's always possible that you'll get a complex question that doesn't tie neatly into a particular theme. The professor may be trying to challenge you—to test your ability to grapple, on the spot, with a very difficult topic. Examine the question and think carefully again about what is being asked. Remember, no matter how confusing the question looks, it must tie in somehow with the subject matter. Remind yourself that because you've spent a great deal of time immersed in this subject, you are equipped to discuss it. Look for any key terms or phrases you understand, and think about the general theme they relate to. You can sometimes discuss the general theme in a very broad sense and still get partial credit.

Whatever you do, make certain you always write *something*. If you at least write some kind of an answer, you might get partial credit. Try to write a confident, well-organized response based on course material, in which you address something that seems related to the question. You'll show the professor you learned something, and this should earn you some credit.

Jot Down a Few Notes

Once you've decided on an essay, jot down a few notes in the margin of the exam booklet on what you plan to address in your response. List the basic points, concepts, key terms, and examples you will raise; if you've identified a general theme that the question relates to, replicate the list of related topics you made at home. If this is not the case, brainstorm for a minute and write down your ideas. Next, consider the order in which you will present them. An essay on an exam is no different from a term paper in that you should be strategic in your organization (we'll discuss term papers more in Chapter 15). Make certain to begin and finish with your most impressive points. But don't spend a great deal of time planning the essay; most of your time should be spent writing.

Neatness Counts—A Lot!

If your professor has to struggle to read your essay, he is not going to view it very positively, even if you've written a brilliant response. That's why, whether it's fair or not, neatness counts. Use a black or blue ink pen, but not one that smudges easily. Only write on one side of a page in the exam booklet, since the ink can show through and make it difficult to read. Most importantly, write as neatly and legibly as possible. If your script is difficult to read, then write in print. It may take you a little longer to print, but your response will be neater and therefore worth the time it takes.

As you are writing, you may find you need to make changes; neatly and clearly cross out a line or a section or add additional information to a previous paragraph. Cross out a section by drawing a line through the material; don't scribble over or blot out what you've written. To add a line or passage, write in the top margin of the page, circle the passage, and draw an arrow down to the spot where it should be inserted.

Communication Is the Key

As you write, remind yourself you are writing for a specific audience with a specific purpose in mind—for your professor, to communicate how much you have learned about the subject. You want to make it crystal clear that you not only learned the material of the course, but also have mastered it as well. That confident attitude should be reflected in the content and style of the essay.

Adopt a tone that indicates your attitude toward the material. Use sophisticated vocabulary and terminology, but not in a forced or incorrect manner. Include as many relevant key terms as possible, along with explanations and definitions. You may even want to underline the key terms, so that they will stand out even if the professor skims the essay. Feel free to be a name-dropper and bring in other sources you may have read. Include as much relevant information as you can that will communicate the breadth of your knowledge and learning.

Be careful as you communicate your thoughts in an essay. Don't, under any circumstances, include anything that is incorrect or that you don't fully understand. If you include any incorrect information, it will make a very poor impression and the professor may penalize you severely, even though other points are correct. You are better off leaving out a particular term or point altogether if your use of it is incorrect. And while you want to convey the breadth of your knowledge, you don't want to pad the essay with irrelevant facts. You can include some that are related, but not central, to the essay, but don't throw in the kitchen sink. Don't bring up topics or terms that have nothing to do with the essay. If you do, the professor will think you don't really understand the question. Include only the points you know are relevant and that will impress the professor.

ALERT

Keep an extra pen out on your desk in case you run out of ink during a test. You don't want to be fumbling in your backpack and calling unnecessary attention to yourself during a test or be possibly viewed as cheating when reaching for your bookbag!

Use a Three-Part Essay Structure

On an exam you don't have much time to plan a detailed, complex structure. You can use the standard three-part structure—the same you would use for a term paper—that includes an introduction, body, and conclusion. This particularly lends itself to examination questions because it provides a set formula. You don't have to think about the organization; you merely plug the relevant information into those three parts.

The Introduction

If the introduction is clear and intelligent, the professor will gain a favorable impression that will remain with him as he continues to read. You don't, however, need to spend a great deal of time writing the introduction. It doesn't have to be especially innovative, creative, or lengthy—it only needs to be a single, short paragraph in which you establish the general topic of the essay. The simplest way to do this is to write a few sentences that essentially rephrase and expand on the question. You should also include a thesis statement that summarizes the central issue of the question. Starting an essay this way not only provides you with material but, more importantly, it gets you writing.

The Body

As with the essay as a whole, it is important the body be well organized and clearly structured. Make certain you divide the body into paragraphs, each centering on a specific point that supports the overall topic of the essay. If you've taken a few moments before the exam to jot down your ideas and plan the order in which you present them, you should be able to write an organized body without too much trouble. It's usually more effective in an exam to include many short paragraphs rather than a few long ones, since it appears you are raising many different points. At the same time, make certain that each paragraph focuses on a very specific concept or example. If you include extraneous information, the essay appears unfocused and sloppy.

The Conclusion

On an exam essay, the conclusion is as important as the introduction. Some professors only skim essays, especially if they have many to grade, but they usually read the introduction and the conclusion, so use these parts to your advantage. While the introduction provides the first impression, the conclusion is the final one your professor gets, and it comes right before he gives your essay a grade. You don't need to have an especially provocative or creative conclusion; you need only summarize the key points within the essay. This will show the professor that you successfully answered the question and know the subject matter.

The conclusion doesn't have to be especially long, either—a few sentences will do. Make certain that you watch the time and leave yourself a few minutes to write it. If the exam ends when you are still working on the body, the essay is essentially unfinished and will appear tentative and unfocused. Adding a short conclusion demonstrates that you had a plan and knew where you were going.

ESSENTIAL

Proofread your work. If necessary, add a caret symbol (^) to insert an extra idea that comes to mind after you review your work. Sometimes having a clearer head helps you to remember other points or ideas.

Watch the Time

Check the time frequently to be certain you have enough time to get all the way through the essay. It's easy to get caught up in a single point, only to find time is running out and you have to rush through the rest of the response. Pace yourself and move quickly by alloting a certain amount of time to address each point and sticking to the schedule. If you are running out of time, finish whatever point you are on and jump ahead to the conclusion. Make certain you include a conclusion, even if it is just a few sentences. In the conclusion, you might refer to some of the additional points you would have made if you had more time. This will at least let the professor know that you are aware of the information.

If you have so little time that you can't complete the essay or write a conclusion, make a brief outline listing the points you planned to address. The professor will see that you do know something about the subject and might give you partial credit. Include a brief note apologizing for not completing the essay because of lack of time. You might get some points for doing this—and every point counts.

After the Exam

Exams can give you valuable insights into your strengths and weaknesses as a test-taker. Whenever possible, examine your tests after they've been graded. If the exam was given during the school semester, your professor will probably give it back to you. If the exam was a final, you may need to make an appointment with the professor and ask to see it. Your finals are especially important in preparing your strategy and course selection for your next semester.

When you get the exam, look through it and study any errors you've made. First, make certain you understand why you got points off. It's particularly important that you do this if later examinations in the semester will cover some of the same material. If you don't get these points right the first time, you're not going to get them right on the final.

You can also try to talk to your professor about the exam. Ask for advice about what you might do in the future to raise your grade. You should talk to the professor particularly if you have failed the exam. By doing this, you demonstrate that you are not a lazy or uncaring student and that you take the course seriously. With luck, the professor might offer valuable advice on how to study that will help you on future tests.

Sometimes teachers make mistakes when they grade exams. If you catch an error, think first about whether it's worth pointing out to the professor. Since you create an unfavorable impression by suggesting their error, it's generally not worth quibbling over a few points. On the other hand, if there was a serious error made in grading your exam, by all means point it out.

If you did poorly or failed, don't get too down about it. Remember this one exam is a small part of a much bigger picture. Later in your life, no one will know what grade you got on a specific test back in school; you probably won't remember it yourself. Try, as much as you can, to turn it into a learning experience; even if you fail a test, you gain some knowledge that can help you in the future.

QUOTE

"I try to read all questions carefully on my tests, making certain I understand them. One trick I enjoy is to try to translate difficult questions into everyday, conversational speech. That way I have a better grasp of what is being asked and how to answer it intelligently."

—Teddy, Junior

CHAPTER 13

Writing Essays: Getting Started

The essence of writing is communication. Writing essays for a class requires you to communicate back concepts you have learned. Both taking tests and writing essays center on how well you communicate. Many people think writing is all about correct grammar and spelling, but an essay can have flawless grammar and still not say anything. In any work of writing, you are communicating your ideas, thoughts, and beliefs to someone in a way that makes them clearly understandable.

Writing Is Communication

The first thing to remember about essay writing is that your goal is to communicate a specific point to an audience. When you are immersed in writing an essay, you can easily forget that you are trying to communicate with a specific person—your teacher, who will grade the essay. You should always keep this in mind: *What can you write that will most impress your teacher?*

A teacher is probably not going to be overly impressed by flawless grammar and spelling; she'll expect those features in a good student's work. What will impress the teacher is the quality and strength of your ideas—those are the crucial components of a good essay. They must be communicated in a manner that makes them accessible to the reader.

Coming up with sophisticated and intelligent ideas is your responsibility; no book can give them to you. This chapter teaches you how to communicate those ideas in such a way that will show them off. Using a step-by-step approach to writing essays, you'll ensure that your ideas are communicated in a clear, organized, and powerful manner.

Finding a Topic

To a large extent, the topic you choose determines the results of the final product. After all, an original and exciting topic will more likely result in an original and exciting essay. You should therefore not choose a topic haphazardly. Your choice of topic must take into account the nature of the assignment and its requirements. Sometimes a teacher will assign a very specific topic and provide you with detailed requirements, specifying exactly what the essay should address. Yet even with the most rigidly defined assignment, you will have room to maneuver. In this case, the challenge is to view the subject from your own point of view and somehow make it your own. You still need to spend time thinking about the assignment and how you plan to approach it in your own individual manner.

At other times, a teacher suggests several topics or provides you with a very loosely defined assignment that gives you a great deal of freedom. Don't make the mistake of thinking that being allowed to choose your own topic makes the essay easier to write. Having free rein with an essay is exciting, but it is also overwhelming. There are so many possibilities for topics; how are you supposed to find one that's right for you?

Consider Your Audience

Good writers always direct their work to the proper audience. For example, you would write a letter requesting a job interview in an entirely different manner than a love letter. In the case of a school essay, your audience will be the teacher who assigned it and will grade it. Before you begin work, make certain you understand the assignment, are aware of the teacher's expectations, and know the exact requirements for the essay. How much research should you be conducting? How long should the essay be? What format should you use? Is there anything specific you should include or address?

ALERT

Don't be afraid to take some risks with your writing. Chances are, your first idea is one many of your classmates have already had, so be original if at all possible. Your work will stand out more and demonstrate to your teacher that you have a voice of your own as well.

You might also want to choose a topic that your teacher will find unique. Many teachers become bored reading about the same topics over and over again; most will therefore welcome a paper written on something unusual. For example, if everyone else in the class is writing about a certain work of literature, then consider choosing a different one. Just make certain that your teacher is open to new ideas and atypical subjects.

It may seem difficult to be original, especially if you are writing about a topic such as a historical event or literary work that has been discussed by others for centuries. The way you approach this topic, though, can add a new twist to it that makes it seem original. If your teacher gives a prompt, then follow it but still try to show some original thought in your work instead of taking a cookie-cutter approach that may look similar to all of your classmates'.

Your writing is one of the most direct forms of communication between you and your teacher. What your teacher sees in your writing contributes significantly to the impression she has of you. An essay that is sloppy and unfocused and filled with typos and grammatical errors paints a portrait of a student who doesn't care that much about what he has submitted. On the other hand, an essay that is neat, well-organized, filled with interesting and original ideas, and carefully proofread indicates that the student takes pride in his work. You can guess which student will get a higher grade on the essay—and for class participation. Remember, your essay tells the teacher a lot more than simply your ideas about a particular subject.

ESSENTIAL

Your writing reflects you; make certain your essay shows you have a serious, professional attitude toward your work.

What Interests You?

If you have a more open-ended assignment with a choice of topics, choose one that, first and foremost, interests you. You are going to spend a great deal of time working on this essay, and if the topic itself doesn't pique your curiosity, those hours will seem even longer and the writing process even more tedious. If you choose a subject you sincerely want to know more about, then the process of researching and writing the essay will be interesting and engaging. Think about the various themes and topics that have been addressed in class, as well as the reading assignments you've completed. Was there a particular subject that you enjoyed learning about? Was there anything you only touched on in class that you wanted to know more about? Did you have an intense emotional reaction to anything? Do you have a particular opinion or point of view about a topic you'd like to express?

Length Requirements

Essays are meant to be detailed, in-depth studies of a particular subject. In order to write a solid, focused essay, you should choose a topic that can be addressed fully and comprehensively within the page requirements set by the teacher.

If you choose a topic that is too broad for the paper's length requirements, you will end up writing about it in simplistic, superficial terms. You won't have the space to get into much detail, so the entire essay will remain on a broad and obvious level. For example, it would be difficult to write an essay on "The Poems of Emily Dickinson" in only six pages; you'd have to discuss each poem in one or two lines in order to address them all. If you choose a more limited topic, such as a common theme in Dickinson's work, and address that in some depth, that may be an easier topic.

ALERT

You can play around with fonts, margin size, and headers and footers once your essay is done. If there is a word-length recommendation, check your word count to be sure you do not exceed it by too much. If you do exceed the recommended word limit, try to keep it minimal. Don't try to make up for a short essay by padding the spacing; your teacher will notice.

Students often initially choose topics that are too broad because they are concerned about meeting the page requirements. At first, six or seven pages sounds like a lot to "fill up," so you might select an extensive topic to guarantee you have enough to write. Once you begin thinking about and researching your topic in depth, however, you'll often find you have plenty of material. In fact, you may find you need to leave some material out.

Yet choosing a topic that is too limited for the page requirements is also a problem. If your topic is too narrow, you may find yourself bending over backwards to meet the page requirements. Your paper then will be wordy and repetitive. For example, it would be difficult to find enough original thoughts to express on a single Emily Dickinson poem in a twenty-five-page essay; you would probably run out of ideas after the first few pages and repeat the same points over and over. Your topic should be broad enough so that you can fill the essay with strong ideas that keep the reader engaged.

Of course, you may not be able to settle on a specific topic right at the start. Don't worry because you do not have to. It's fine to begin with a broad, general topic and then gradually narrow it down until you hit upon a topic appropriate for the length of your essay.

A Place to Start

Here is a list of general topics that would make a good starting point for researching an essay:

- A particular work of literature, article or text, or a body of works
- An author, person, or a particular group of individuals
- A historical period or event, or a contemporary news event
- A literary period or genre
- A scientific field or subfield, in either the general sciences or social sciences
- A particular issue or subject of debate, either historical or contemporary

All of the above are broad subjects that would take lengthy papers to fully examine them. They all make fine *starting* points for selecting an essay topic; you can choose one and begin to think and read more about it. As you do, you'll gradually be able to narrow it down to a topic appropriate for the length of your essay.

Read, Think, Percolate

After you've chosen a general topic, immerse yourself in the subject matter by reading and thinking about it at great length. Doing this, you learn more about the subject and generate ideas to use in your essay. You also begin to narrow the general topic down to a more specific one.

Start by reading anything you can find that relates to your chosen subject. You can begin with online search engines. You can, for example, consult a general online encyclopedia to see if there is an entry relating to your topic. Make certain you pick a thorough, academic encyclopedia such as *Encyclopaedia Britannica*, *Encyclopedia Americana*, or *Collier's Encyclopedia*. You can also find many specialized dictionaries and encyclopedias that address specific fields.

Next, search the stacks of the library for general books on your topic. Use the library's online search program and search according to the subject. Pick books that look promising and copy down their call numbers. All of the books related to that subject should be located in the same section of the library, so you can go to that section and browse. Select a few books that seem interesting and read sections of them. You don't necessarily need to read the entire book. For example, reading the introduction to a book on your topic may provide you with a great deal of information.

You can also do a similar type of research at your local bookstore. Grab a notebook or your laptop and hang out in the aisle where your topic is grouped.

If you are writing an essay that centers on a specific text, such as a particular book or article, it is crucial that you reread that text several times. As you read, jot down any ideas that pop into your head that might make a contribution to an essay. Reading the text a few times may provide you with enough ideas to get started on your essay. Don't expect the ideas to happen right away. The mind needs to let information percolate for a while. Soon, you'll begin making connections with things you've learned, forming your own opinions, and gaining insight into the material. As you continue reading, your ideas and interests will become more focused and defined, and you will be able to narrow down your topic. Although you don't have to concern yourself just yet with taking detailed notes, remember to make a note of any ideas that pop into your head.

Creating a Thesis Statement

The key to any essay is its thesis statement. The thesis statement is the paper's central idea; it functions as the essay's backbone, holding together the various parts as a cohesive whole.

The thesis statement is not the same thing as your topic, although they are closely related. Your topic is a general subject that you've read and thought about to generate specific ideas. Based on that process, you should now be able to formulate a particular point of view about some aspect of the topic. This viewpoint, condensed into a single sentence that sums up the central idea of the essay, is your thesis statement.

Every essay should have a thesis statement and all ideas expressed in the paper should reflect it. Without the thesis statement, the essay is merely a random list of ideas, without any clear, definable point.

A thesis statement can simply be a sentence that presents the central topic of the paper. Starting with this basic statement results in a straightforward essay that summarizes aspects of the subject matter. A more effective thesis statement reflects a specific viewpoint or opinion about the subject matter; the essay, in turn, represents the detailed argument that supports this viewpoint. Most teachers prefer this kind of essay; they are interested in your own perspective, rather than a summary of factual information. The more original the thesis statement, the more original—and impressive—your essay will be.

Here are some sample topics and the effective thesis statements that might emerge from them.

Topics	Thesis Statements
American Literature of the 1920s	Most American literature of the 1920s depicts a growing anxiety regarding the dehumanizing effects of industrialization.
Modern Psychological Theories and Treatments	Although dreams play a central role in both Freudian and Jungian theory, there are crucial differences in the ways in which dreams are interpreted.
The Cold War	The foreign policy of the United States during the Cold War indirectly served to escalate domestic problems on American soil.

In order for a thesis statement to be effective, it should be specific and reflect your own ideas. It should:

- **Be specific.** An effective thesis statement is not too broad or general; instead, it should say something very specific about your topic. By being very specific, a thesis statement ensures that the essay remains focused and does not veer off into unrelated territory that distracts the reader.
- **Reflect your own ideas.** Most professors will be more impressed when you express your own thoughts and ideas rather than regurgitating someone else's. A more effective thesis statement will therefore be original and reflect your own outlook on the subject. Make certain the thesis is phrased entirely in your own words.

- **Be something you believe.** The body of the essay must make a convincing argument supporting the thesis statement. It is extremely difficult to present a solid argument supporting an idea that you don't actually believe is true. Moreover, if the thesis statement reflects a personal belief, the entire essay will bear the strength of your convictions. Don't work against the grain and choose a thesis statement that you don't support.

- **Be something you can build a solid argument to support.** Your goal in writing the essay is to convince your reader that your thesis statement is an accurate one; you want to prove your viewpoint beyond a shadow of a doubt. So, make certain you pick a thesis you know you can prove. When you actually begin conducting research, you may find you don't necessarily agree with it or that you cannot prove it. If that happens, change the thesis statement.

- **Be a single, direct sentence.** Most essays for academic purposes are limited in length; you probably won't have to write a book-length dissertation. You therefore don't need a long, detailed thesis statement. Make certain you can phrase your thesis statement in one sentence. If you can't do it in one sentence, it indicates you are unfocused and confused about your idea, or that you've chosen a thesis too ambitious to be proven in a single essay.

ESSENTIAL

Once you have an idea of what your thesis statement will be, discuss it with your teacher. This will assure you that you are on the right track. Your teacher may also have suggestions on how to conduct research and organize the essay.

You may need to fine-tune your thesis statement. Until you've actually begun writing, it is fine to have only a general sense of your thesis. As you conduct research and gain more knowledge of your topic, you'll continue to hone your thesis statement.

Choosing a Title

Students often fail to put titles on their essays, but the title, which indicates the general topic, is an important component. It can also give the reader a first impression of the writer. Try to brainstorm a title that conveys information about the essay but is also intelligent and witty. One effective strategy is to use a title and subtitle, separated by a colon. The title should be a short phrase or quotation; the subtitle that follows should be a longer phrase or a sentence that explains the essay's topic in more detail. For example:

- Open for Business: The Portrayal of Commerce and Economics in the First Scene of Shakespeare's *Merchant of Venice*
- "I'll Talk About Anything I Want to, George": Vying for Control of Conversation in Edward Albee's *Who's Afraid of Virginia Woolf?*

When writing titles, remember:

- Capitalize the first letters of the first and last word.
- Capitalize the first letters of all words in the title except for articles, prepositions, and conjunctions.
- Never put the entire title in quotation marks. A caveat: If there is a quoted phrase within the title, you should put that in quotation marks.
- Never italicize the entire title. If you mention the title of a major work within the title, though, you should italicize that.
- Never punctuate the title with a period.

Getting Started

One of the more difficult aspects of crafting an essay is actually beginning to write. Even after all the research, it can be very intimidating to sit down and start writing. Part of the difficulty comes from the way many students tend to view writing. Students don't think of writing as a process, and only value the finished product—which is supposed to be flawless. This thinking, however, places tremendous pressure on you. If you think the writing needs to be perfect, you might freeze up with panic, afraid to commit yourself to a single word on paper.

Finding Your Voice

Regardless of whether or not you are required to conduct research, the heart of the essay should be your own ideas. As you refine your ideas, your own voice and style will emerge. In the course of researching and thinking about your topic, you will develop certain ideas and a sense of the major points you want to make. These ideas will still be in your head, where they are probably mixed together. In order to be a compelling, powerful essay, these ideas need to be organized in a logical manner. You need to get them out on paper, so you can examine them and plan a strategic way to address them in the essay.

ESSENTIAL

Your writing should sound like you speaking to your reader. (Though, obviously the words "um," 'like," or other stumbling words do not appear!) Your reader should be comfortable hearing you through your words, though. Using a sense of humor in your writing can also be effective and welcome when appropriate.

Writing Style

Every piece of writing has its own distinctive style. The style reflects the manner in which something is written, and depends on such factors as the choice of words, sentence patterns, and the way ideas are introduced. An essay's style indicates the writer's attitude toward the material, and signals to the reader how to respond. For example, the style can indicate if a work is serious, sarcastic, humorous, or silly.

ALERT

Be careful about addressing your reader or the teacher directly in your writing. While your tone can be friendly, actually saying the words "you" or "reader" or asking the reader a direct question is not usually a good idea.

When you are writing an academic essay, you generally want to use a serious, intelligent style. Avoid being too chatty or conversational. Avoid using slang or casual expressions; instead, use a sophisticated but realistic vocabulary. Write sentences that are more varied and complex in structure than "See Dick run." At the same time, don't overdo it. If you try too hard to write in an academic manner, the essay might become too stilted or confusing.

Good writing takes time and effort to produce. You can't expect to get the essay right on the first try; in fact, you shouldn't even try. Instead, it's better to write in stages, making changes and improvements with each draft.

QUOTE

"The process of writing has been just that: a process. I take calculated steps to follow a format that makes my writing appear clear, strong, and understood by my intelligent audience."

—Jim L., Sophomore

CHAPTER 14

Becoming a Great Researcher

Researching for an essay or paper can be a painstaking and tedious process. It can also be very rewarding if you think of yourself as an investigator trying to find clues to help sort out your assignment. Being a researcher means you seek ideas of others to confirm or deny your thesis statement or assigned topic. You become part of a much bigger world of academia once you research a project or paper. The strategies presented in this chapter provide you with the tools you need to be successful in your quest.

Research Sources

There are essentially two kinds of essays: those that require you to do research from outside sources, and ones that do not. Essays that do not require research focus solely on your own thoughts and ideas about a particular topic; those that include research utilize information from outside sources to explain and support your thesis. Your teacher will tell you whether or not you are expected to do research and include other sources in your essay. If the teacher doesn't tell you, then ask.

ALERT

Think of research as detective work. You are essentially investigating your topic in search of clues to reach a result (your final project). Using quotes, facts, and other informative nuggets in your writing clue your reader into your process and investigative expertise.

There are two kinds of sources: *primary* and *secondary*. Primary sources are any texts that are the focus of an essay, such as specific works of literature, historical documents, or essays and articles that present certain theories and philosophies. For example, if you are writing about some of Shakespeare's plays, then *Romeo and Juliet* and *Hamlet* would be primary sources. If your essay centers on a primary source, you must make certain you read it in detail and take notes on it.

Many essays also incorporate secondary sources. These are books and articles by critics, historians, scholars, and other writers who comment on and address primary sources, as well as other topics and subjects. If your essay involves conducting research, you need to track down secondary sources that address your topic and take notes on them.

Where to Find Possible Sources

There are obviously many sources that address your topic, but before you read them, you need to find them. Fortunately, there are several resources you can turn to for help in finding possible sources:

The Online Library Catalog

Unless you are researching in a very antiquated or elementary library that uses old-fashioned card catalogs only, most all libraries nowadays list their sources on computer. The entries are usually organized four ways: by author, title, subject, or keywords. If you have a specific source in mind, you can consult either the author or title entries to find out if the library has the source and where it is located. If you are merely looking for general sources, though, you can search according to the subject.

Most libraries organize their subject catalogs according to the standard list of subjects set by the Library of Congress, although some libraries have their own classifications. The library should have a subject list available for you to consult. Sometimes a subject will be divided into subcategories. Try to find whatever subject or subcategory most closely relates to your topic.

Published Bibliographies and Indexes

There are many published bibliographies and indexes that list books and other sources, such as academic journals and periodic articles, on a particular subject. These bibliographies compile citations for various books and sources. A citation is a listing for a particular source that includes key information about the book, such as the author, title, publisher, and often a brief summary of the source's content.

Here are some of the major bibliographies that might be helpful in your search for sources.

GENERAL SOURCES
- *Books in Print*
- *Essay and General Literature Index*
- *Reader's Guide to Periodical Literature*

ARTS, HUMANITIES, AND LITERATURE
- *Annual Bibliography of English Language and Literature*
- *Humanities Index*
- *MLA International Bibliography of Books and Articles on the Modern Languages and Literatures*

BIOGRAPHY
- *Biography and Genealogy Master Index*
- *Biography Index*
- *Who's Who*

HISTORY
- *Historical Abstracts*
- *International Bibliography of Historical Sciences*

CURRENT EVENTS
- *Facts on File*
- Newspaper Indexes (check for specific newspapers such as the *New York Times,* the *Wall Street Journal,* etc.).

SCIENCES
- *General Science Index*
- *Social Sciences Index*

Bibliographies and indexes will usually be located in the reference section of the library. To find a bibliography on your topic, you can either ask the librarian for suggestions or consult the online subject catalog.

Lists of Works Cited and Bibliographies in Sources

Most academic books, essays, and journals include their own bibliographies, list of works cited, or suggested further readings. These listings provide sources you might read yourself as part of your research. Each time you read a new book or article, check the author's bibliography or notes to see if there is anything of interest that you can explore next. You can also check the assigned texts for your course.

Computerized Information Resources

Most of the indexes listed above, such as the *MLA Bibliography* and the *Reader's Guide to Periodic Literature,* are available via computer catalog or Internet. All libraries have computers set up that enable you to conduct online searches or allow you to log into their city's wireless via your own laptop.

Obviously, the Internet is a valuable tool for finding sources. You can access indexes and bibliographies, and also find entire articles from newspapers, magazines, and periodicals. Just be careful of Googling every question you have and relying on Wikipedia for your sources of knowledge. Wikipedia is an open site that allows information to be updated and changed rather easily, so be sure you are certain about information you think may be factual but can actually be edited by the public.

ALERT

Be cautious about including information you find on sites like Wikipedia. Double check sources and facts you find there. Since Wikipedia is a database of millions of articles that can be updated and edited by anyone with Internet access, be cautious of believing the entire content as truth or fact.

Use Google, Yahoo, Alta Vista, or other search engines as a place to start for database searches, but be sure your sources are reliable before citing them in your research.

The Librarian

Librarians are the most vital resource in the library; they can provide you with a tremendous amount of help for just about any academic project you pursue. Ask them questions; that's what they're there for. Any good library should offer some, if not all, of the above resources and services. It's a good idea to wander around your library or take a brief tour to find out exactly what the library offers. Then take advantage of it. If you use the library properly, its resources can make the job of being a student much, much easier.

ESSENTIAL

Become familiar with your library, not just as a quiet space where you can study, but also as a source of information. Finding the perfect quote or just the right reference source can be very exciting and empowering as you achieve academic success.

When a book is located in the reference section, you will not be allowed to take it out of the library. You'll have to photocopy relevant sections or sit in the library and take notes on the source. The advantage, though, is that you know the books will always be there.

In addition to books, libraries house many other research materials, including magazines, newspapers, journals, videotapes, audiotapes, and maps. These materials are usually kept within their own rooms or sections. You can ask the librarian or check the library directory to find where these sections are.

Magazines, periodicals, and scholarly journals are sometimes bound together in volumes and shelved in the stacks. This is why bibliographies list a volume number in addition to the date of a particular periodical. But, due to the enormous space newspapers and magazines take up, as well as the problem of decay, libraries only keep them for a limited time period and most of the outdated paper publications are available electronically via computer. Librarians can assist you with online research beyond the usual Google or Yahoo search engines. Westlaw, LexisNexis, and other academic or scholarly search engines, as well as online databases, may offer more in-depth or subject specific research opportunities for your project or assignment.

Keeping Track of Sources

It is important to know how to categorize and document all of your sources when conducting research. You also need to stay organized and have a good system in place to keep track of all the places from where you gather your information. This system ultimately will protect you from the threat of committing plagiarism, whether accidental or intentional.

Citing Sources

Whenever you find a reference to a source you'd like to investigate, make a note of it. It is extremely important that you write down all relevant information: the author(s), title, publisher (for a book); volume and date (for a periodical or journal); or anthology name and editor (for an essay or article included in another work). This information helps you to find the source and is also necessary when you create your own bibliography. You can keep this information in a notebook, on a legal pad, or in a file on your laptop.

Tracking Down Sources

Once you've discovered a source, you then need to track it down. Use the best library that is available to you. A college or university library will probably have a more extensive collection and better resources than a local public library. The main branch of the public library in most cities will have a large collection of sources and varied services.

The bulk of the library's resources consists of books that are shelved in the "stacks." If you are looking for a book, simply check the library's catalog to find the call number. The first few digits of the call number will generally indicate the subject and general section of the library housing the book, while the last few digits indicate the specific book. Using the call number, you can find the exact shelf where a book should be located. You then just need to match the call number you've written down to the one on the spine to find the right book. If you aren't certain where to look, ask the librarian.

At most libraries, the public is allowed access to the stacks. You can freely look through the shelves for books you want to take out. At some, however, you will need to fill out a request slip with the call number and give it to the librarian. The book will then be retrieved for you.

Of course, a particular book is not always going to be on the shelf. It might be lost or taken out by someone else. If this is the case, go to the circulation desk and tell them which source you need. They can often tell you when the book is due back and put a hold on it so it will be reserved for you once it is returned. If the book is missing, they can place a search on it. Unfortunately, a book search is going to have limited results; if the book is missing, you should probably assume it is not going to be found and look for other sources.

If the library doesn't have a particular source, don't despair. Many libraries provide an interlibrary loan service. Ask at the circulation desk or in the reference library what you need to do to get a book through this service. Other online sources are also available by searching Wikipedia's list of academic databases and search engines or their list of online databases.

Taking Notes

When you are reading a particular source, you may not be certain what to take notes on. Sources can be quite long; how do you know what is relevant and what isn't? The most important things to look for are anything that supports your thesis statement. Essentially, you are looking for hard evidence that argues in favor of your thesis. You can also take notes on anything that relates to your general topic, since these notes will help you develop broad background knowledge of the field and might be used in the essay. Also, take notes on anything that intrigues you or sounds interesting. You won't necessarily use all of these notes in the essay, but it is much easier to take notes and throw them out later than have to reread sources.

As You Narrow Your Topic

In the initial stages of research, you may not have formulated your thesis entirely or conceived of the overall points your essay will make. You therefore may be uncertain about what notes to take. It can be helpful to read a sampling of the sources you've tracked down before beginning to take notes. This will enable you to develop a background knowledge in the subject, which in turn will help you fine-tune your thesis. When you have a better idea of the shape of your essay, you can then go back to various sources, read them carefully, and take notes.

By the way, if your essay utilizes primary sources, you need to read these carefully and take notes on them as well. Notes and quotations from primary sources are particularly strong pieces of evidence, especially if a primary source is the focus of your essay.

Writing Down Specific Information Properly

There are two types of notes: *quotations* and *paraphrases*. A quotation restates a passage or a part of a passage from a source in the original writer's *exact* words. A paraphrase, on the other hand, restates the ideas in a passage rephrased in *your own* words.

Quoting

When you are reading a source and come across a sentence or passage you think is relevant, decide whether you want to quote it or paraphrase it.

You should generally paraphrase more often than you quote. It is too tedious and time-consuming to copy down long passages word for word. If a sentence or passage is written in a particularly interesting or powerful manner that you think will stand well on its own in the essay however, then copy it as a quotation.

Be certain you put copied lines in quotation marks. To be certain you remember that the note is a quotation, you may even want to write "Quotation from Original" next to the line in parentheses. If you want to leave out part of a quotation because it is not relevant, you can use an *ellipsis* to indicate a word or phrase has been deleted. An ellipsis consists of either three spaced periods if the omission is within a sentence, or four spaced periods if the omission comes at the end of a sentence. Sometimes, when you take a quotation out of context, it won't make sense on its own and will need some clarification. If you decide to add a word or phrase to the quotation, you must put it in brackets to indicate that the addition is not part of the quotation.

Paraphrasing

If you decide to paraphrase the source, you must rephrase it *completely in your own words*. Make certain that your paraphrase is an accurate restatement of the passage.

Occasionally, you will want to quote a few words or a particular phrase within a paraphrase. You can paraphrase the gist of the passage and include only a few words and phrases in quotation marks. For example, if the author has coined a particular term or described something in a unique way, you can quote those words exactly.

ESSENTIAL

There are many ways to take notes. The simplest method is to use a notebook or legal pad as you read. Some students prefer to take notes directly onto a laptop or desktop computer. Find a system that works for you. Remember to indicate clearly which source the notes come from and their page numbers.

Whenever you take quotes from a source, and even if you paraphrase them, you need to note the source and its exact page number(s). It is important that you do this carefully, as you must include this information later in the essay. If you don't acknowledge the original source, you are committing *plagiarism*, which is considered a serious breach of ethics that can get you expelled from school.

Using Note Cards

If you are utilizing many sources and taking many notes, the material can become difficult to manage. A more efficient and organized means of taking notes is to use note cards. These give you more flexibility—you can shuffle and reorganize them into various groups, or put aside those you decide not to use.

Take notes on index cards (you may want to use a slightly larger size, such as 4" × 6", so you can fit more notes). On each card, write down a particular piece of information from one specific source. Each card should contain a single, specific idea. Copying lengthy quotations and paraphrasing large chunks of text take away the flexibility that note cards provide you with in the first place. Try to limit each card to a single point.

ALERT

Keep careful records with complete publication information of all your sources. In order to credit the sources, you need to place a "works cited" page at the end of your essay that includes all this information. Using works cited note cards is the most efficient way to keep track of sources. Simply keep one notecard per source, complete with all its bibliographic information. Alphabetize them at the end and format properly depending on the type of publication source it is: a book, website, periodical, speech, etc.

As long as you have made a works cited card, you don't need to put the full title and complete publication information on each note card. Simply copy down the last name of the author in the upper left-hand corner of the card. If you are using more than one source by a particular writer, you can write down the author's last name and a key word from the title. In the top right-hand corner, write down the exact page number from which the noted quotation or paraphrase comes.

To ensure that you distinguish between quotations and paraphrases, you may want to write on the card in big, block letters "QUOTATION" or "PARAPHRASE."

Sample Note Card

Stevens, Shakespeare   *p. 42*

Productions of Shakespeare in the 1990s change the scene or time period. Sometimes the change is positive and adds something, but at others it only makes things confusing. (PARAPHRASE)

Generate Your Own Ideas

Regardless of whether or not you are required to conduct research, the heart of the essay should be your own ideas. Jot down your ideas before you actually begin writing the essay. In the course of researching and thinking about your topic, you will develop certain ideas and a sense of the major points you want to make. These ideas, though, will still be in your head, where they are probably mixed together. In order to be a compelling, powerful essay, you need to organize the ideas in a logical manner. You need to get them out on paper (or a computer screen), so you can examine them and plan a strategic way to address them in the essay.

The writing process is like brainstorming; as you write about one particular idea or point, you'll probably find yourself conceiving of many additional ones. You don't need to worry about things like grammar, spelling, format, or structure when you write down your ideas; you don't even have to write in complete sentences. Just write anything that comes to mind in relation to the topic. You can then refer to these notes—along with any notes from additional sources if this is a research paper—as you organize your essay.

When you are finished jotting down your ideas, read them over and transfer the major ones onto note cards. You can play around with how you organize them in this form, and also integrate them with the note cards from outside sources.

> **Sample Note Card of Original Ideas**
> *My Idea for Essay*
> *Cycles and Repetitions in LDJ.*
> *There are lots of images that are repeated throughout Long Day's Journey.*
> *— family mealtimes*
> *— cycle of time; one day after another (implied in the title)*
> *— drinking from the bottle then filling with water*
> *— men leaving Mary alone on-stage*

Write a key word or phrase to describe each category on index cards to identify each group. If a card seems to belong in more than one group, place it in the one that seems most applicable; however, write a note on the card indicating other categories it relates to.

After going through your notes, you'll have several piles of note cards made up of various categories and subcategories of notes. Each group represents a point you plan to make in the essay. You need to decide next on the order in which you will address these points.

The strategy of your essay is a personal decision. Different writers have their own favorite strategic devices and techniques. Additionally, each essay has its own specific strategy and logic. Before you start writing, consider the overall effect you want to create and conceive of a strategy that achieves it.

Plagiarism 101

As you research and generate your own ideas, it's vital to avoid plagiarism. Whenever one writer uses another writer's ideas or words and does not give the original writer credit, it is considered plagiarism. Plagiarism is like stealing. Committing plagiarism is a breach of ethics that can have serious repercussions for a student, including a failing grade or being expelled.

The most blatant form of plagiarism is copying an entire essay from another student or source. It is also considered plagiarism if you include information from another source within your essay and don't credit the source.

Even one uncredited sentence or phrase can be considered plagiarism. You probably won't be expelled over one or two uncredited sentences, but failing to document sources can lower your grade or discredit you as a student.

ALERT

Committing plagiarism is an infraction that can haunt your academic record and academic reputation for years and often becomes a part of your permanent academic record. It is so much better to be conservative and cite anything that is not your own work, idea, or quotation than to risk getting tagged as a plagiarist.

When you are assigned an essay that requires research, you are obviously allowed to consult sources. You just need to be very careful that you always give credit to these sources whenever you use them. As you might imagine, quoting from, paraphrasing, and crediting sources can become quite messy, especially if you aren't consistent about the way you do it. To help make essays readable, standard formats have been developed to provide consistency within an essay and from one essay to another. Ask your professor which format to use and make certain you follow it. The most popular currently used in most schools are those developed by the Modern Language Association (MLA) and American Psychological Association (APA), and known as the MLA and APA formats. You can purchase a handbook for either one.

In general, these standard formats consist of two components: citations within the essay and the list of works cited at the essay's conclusion. Whenever you quote or paraphrase a source, include a citation with the sentence or passage that indicates which source it comes from, as well as the page number within the source. These citations are usually abbreviations for the whole source, such as the author's last name or a key word in the source's title. The citation corresponds to a listing in the Works Cited section, at the end of the essay, where the full publication information for each source is listed. There are specific formats for listing different types of sources in the Works Cited section. Your professor will specify a specific format, and you can purchase a handbook to help you with it. Remember, always give credit where credit is due.

QUOTE

"Researching at the library has become one of my favorite tasks. Internet research, while speedy and instant, has often gotten me into some trouble in terms of confirming the validity and truth of my sources. I feel that the good, old-fashioned brick-and-mortar library is a haven for me to explore to my heart's content. It is all there for me to find."

—Stone J., Freshman

CHAPTER 15

Finally: Writing Your Essay

Before lawyers go to court, they carefully prepare how they intend to present their evidence. They think about the order in which they plan to call up witnesses and the particular lines of questioning they will follow. Planning ahead in this way guarantees an organized and strategically effective presentation of the case. Your essay similarly represents an argument—this one in support of your thesis. You also need to plan ahead, organizing your evidence and devising a presentation strategy.

Plan Your Attack

The first thing to do is to read through and evaluate all your notes. Decide which notes are necessary for your argument. *Everything in the final essay must relate to the thesis statement.* You may ultimately decide to put many unrelated notes aside; don't let this bother you. By evaluating notes in a critical manner, only the most powerful material remains. Information that doesn't contribute significantly weighs down the essay and detracts from the stronger ideas.

As you work, keep your own ideas in mind. You may want to use them as the basis for grouping together the themes. Each group of note cards you wrote represents a point you plan to make in the essay. You need to decide next on the order in which you will address these points. Many students follow some variation of the following steps of the writing process.

Brainstorm

You can brainstorm on a blank sheet of paper or computer screen some of your ideas and see how they come together. Some students like to "cluster" to come up with a more formal outline. "Clustering" is a visual way of mapping out your future essay. If your essay is about water, for instance, write the word "water" in the center of a page. Then, branching out around it like the rays of a sun, write various words or terms that support, define, or relate to the topic of water.

Another technique that can get your structure on paper is freewriting. That is simply a stream-of-consciousness way to get ideas down as they jump into your head. Ignoring sentence structure, grammar, and spelling, just write without stopping until you empty your head of your ideas for your essay.

Start an Outline

In planning your essay, it helps to make a rough outline. The outline simply lists the major points of the essay, and the smaller topics and issues that relate to each one, in the order in which you plan to address them. This gives you a clear map to follow when you sit down to write. Like all good maps, it will keep you from getting lost.

Try to include as much detail as possible within the rough outline. The more specifics you include, the more organized you'll be. Beneath the general categories in the outline, you can mention specific notes from sources you plan to use; you might even want to write out or sum up specific quotations.

When organizing your points, make certain that you order them in a logical fashion. You want one point to lead to the next, so that the reader will be able to follow your argument without having to fill in gaps. Certain categories of notes should follow one another.

The order in which you raise points can influence the effect they have on your reader. In evaluating your different notes—your pieces of "evidence"—you've probably become aware that certain ones are much more powerful than others. Consider how to order your points so that the most persuasive ones pack the most punch. Strategically, you may want to build up to your most powerful point so you make a strong last impression on your reader. At the same time, you don't want to start off with a weak point that will make a poor first impression.

Remember that this rough outline is not written in stone; you can make changes at any time. In the process of writing the essay, or after you've read over early drafts of it, you may find that certain points work better if addressed in a different place. You can make as many changes as you like, provided that everything in the essay still relates to the thesis.

Write the First Draft

Good writing takes time and effort to produce. You can't expect to get the essay right on the first try and, in fact, you shouldn't even try. Instead, it's better to write in stages, making changes and improvements with each draft.

The most important goal of a rough draft is to get all your ideas on paper and to integrate them with notes from other sources. Correct grammar and spelling are important parts of an essay because they help make it understandable and readable. Don't concern yourself with this in your first draft, though. This eliminates a great deal of the stress about writing; you don't have to think about the "rules" at first and can simply concentrate on conveying your ideas.

Start at the beginning of the rough outline and simply start writing. Do your best to explain each of the points. As you need to, refer to your notes and include quotations or paraphrases from other sources. Make certain you add citations for each sentence that include information from another source. Keep on writing until you've reached the end of the rough outline. Don't stop to go back or make changes. If you hit a roadblock—a point when you freeze and don't know how to proceed—mark the place with an X and move on to another point. You can go back to the trouble spot later.

This first draft will be extremely rough; the writing will be choppy and difficult to read. But that's okay—it's only the first draft and you are the only one who has to see it. This draft provides you with the raw material for your essay; you can then work on it and refine it until it is a real gem.

Basic Five-Paragraph Essay Structure

Although there are many ways to structure an essay, the most basic is the five-paragraph structure that includes an introduction with thesis statement, three supporting paragraphs, and conclusion. It is not a law that you have to use this structure for everything you write. You might, for example, have a teacher who is open to more loosely structured essays and who encourages you to be creative. Regardless, this structure is a basic fundamental formula that if you master it can take you through high school and college quite effectively. It ensures that the essay remains focused on a specific point and that ideas are presented in a logical and organized fashion. Following this structure, especially when you are first learning how to write academic essays, will help you write more persuasively.

The Introduction

The introduction, at the beginning of the essay, is where you introduce your general topic, specific thesis statement, and approach or methodology. For most essays, the introduction only needs to be a single, well-written paragraph. By being succinct, the introduction has more impact.

The introduction should draw your reader into your argument right away. It functions somewhat like a movie preview, to give your audience a taste of what's to come, but not the whole story. You want your reader to be enticed and interested in what you have to say.

ALERT

In bigger projects or longer writing assignments, ones that are more than twenty pages, such as an honors thesis or dissertation, the introduction can be somewhat longer than just a paragraph since there is more ground to cover and a larger set of topics to introduce.

Because the thesis statement is central to the essay, it is an important part of the introduction. You generally can't begin an essay with the thesis statement itself, because it represents a specific point of view about a broader subject. The introduction sets up the thesis by presenting general background information that gives it a context.

Begin the introductory paragraph with a broad, general statement about the paper's topic or even a question. Try to have it be interesting and catchy to encourage your reader to want more information. Remember that the first few sentences give the reader the first impression of your essay; it is extremely important that you make a good first impression. The first sentences should be well written, interesting, and, most important, give the reader some idea of the paper's topic. The rest of the introduction then bridges the opening statement with the thesis statement, which is usually the last sentence of the introduction. You should indicate how you plan to approach your argument and the kinds of sources that will serve as your evidence. If you plan on looking at specific examples to prove the thesis, you can identify these cases also.

The introduction is the first and possibly only place in the essay where you spell out the thesis statement directly for the reader. You therefore need to be careful about how you word it. You don't want it to be too fancy, flashy, or wordy; the power of the idea should be enough to impress the reader. Just state it in a direct, unambiguous manner.

The introduction should come entirely from you. In general, it is not the place to quote and paraphrase outside sources. Those sources belong in the body of the paper, where you use them to prove the thesis statement. It wouldn't make any sense to discuss such specific sources before you've even stated the argument of the essay. Moreover, you want the reader to be primarily impressed by the power of your own ideas.

ESSENTIAL

Look on your bookshelf at classic titles or go online to read the opening phrases of celebrated books for inspiration on how to begin your paper or assignment. Don't be afraid to take risks in finding creative ways to hook your reader.

You can also occasionally begin an essay with a quotation from another source or by mentioning a specific source; you should only do this if the quotation or source is obviously closely connected to your thesis statement. If the quotation or source introduces specific issues, you probably should not raise it this early in the essay. If you want to be a bit more creative with the introduction and you think your teacher is open to this kind of writing, you might start the essay with a brief observation or question that connects with your topic. Just remember that the introduction should always alert the reader to your general topic, your approach or methodology, and your thesis statement.

The Body

The body is the bulk of your essay; this is where you present your detailed argument that supports the thesis statement. After having conducted research and thought at length about your topic, you should have several points to make. You will therefore use the body to present your ideas in as clear and organized a fashion as possible.

If you have conducted research from primary or secondary sources, you can quote and paraphrase from these sources extensively in this section. Information that comes from other sources serves as strong evidence, but take care to distinguish your own ideas from those in other sources. Quotations and paraphrases should only be brought into the essay to lend credence to your ideas. Whenever you introduce information from another source, you should explain exactly how it fits in with your own point. And always make certain that each time you quote or paraphrase an outside source, you formally credit the source using the *Modern Language Association* (MLA) *Handbook* as your reference for proper formatting and crediting of sources.

Following are three important components of a well-written body.

The Material Clearly Relates to the Thesis Statement

The most important thing to keep in mind when writing the body is that every bit of information you include should relate to the thesis and you must spell out exactly how it does. If something doesn't relate to the thesis, get rid of it; it's only clouding up your argument, serving as "fluffy" writing, and detracting from its power.

Your Arguments Are Complete

Because your ideas make sense to you, you may think you have fully explained them, when in fact you haven't done so in a manner that someone else can understand. The reader cannot see inside your head. You must therefore explain all your points carefully, making them clear to the reader. Don't worry at first if it seems that you are overexplaining your points and ideas. It may seem that way to you, but a reader requires a more detailed explanation in order to understand your points as clearly as you do. If you find repetition later upon reading over your draft, you can trim at that point.

The Writing Flows Smoothly

As the writer of the essay, it's your job to act as the guide for the reader. As you ease the reader through the complexities of your argument, journeying from one point to the next, you want to create as smooth a path as possible, so that by the end of the essay, the reader won't feel disoriented. At times, you need to make it clear exactly where the essay is heading or summarize what has already been demonstrated. You also don't want the paper to be choppy or difficult to read. Instead, one idea or point should flow smoothly into the next.

One way you can ensure the paper is clearly organized is by focusing each paragraph around a specific point. The body should always be written in paragraphs, not in one long chunk of text. Each paragraph should focus upon a specific point, and every sentence in that paragraph should relate to it. Any sentence in the paragraph that doesn't should be taken out. It's also a good idea to begin each paragraph with a topic sentence that generally introduces the subject matter or main idea of the paragraph. The topic sentence can also serve as a transition between ideas, demonstrating how the next paragraph builds on, contrasts, or departs from the previous one.

FACT

As you write, make sure your paragraphs aren't too long. Long paragraphs weigh down your reader and can be tedious if you drone on and on about a supporting idea. Sprinkle in quotes or even a question to help provide a pause.

Each sentence and paragraph in the body should flow smoothly and logically from one to the next. Use transitional words and phrases in certain sentences, particularly topic sentences, so that your reader can easily follow how different points are related to one another. There are many transitional words and phrases you can use to connect various sentences and paragraphs, including these:

- To build upon a previous sentence or paragraph: *and, also, additionally, as a result, consequently, further, furthermore, in addition, moreover*
- To compare with a previous sentence or paragraph: *similarly, in the same manner, likewise, at the same time, by the same token*
- To contrast with a previous sentence or paragraph: *however, but, in contrast, nevertheless, although, yet, on the other hand*
- To summarize or draw a conclusion: *therefore, in other words, in short, to sum up, thus*

The Conclusion

After reading the body and all the evidence you've presented in support of the thesis, the reader should now view the thesis statement not as conjecture but as a claim that is supported. That's exactly what you express in the conclusion. The conclusion is essentially the mirror image of the introduction, but one that stresses the fact that the thesis has now been proven. The conclusion should therefore refer to the thesis statement in some form, and affirm that it has been proven and supported. You should also recap the major points you've made in the paper to establish your argument.

Like the introduction, the conclusion for most essays only needs to be one paragraph and it should primarily represent your own words and ideas. This is also not a place to quote or paraphrase extensively from secondary sources.

ESSENTIAL

While the introduction contributes to the reader's first impression of your essay, the conclusion will influence the reader's final impression. You want to end with a bang—with some of your most powerful and dramatic writing—that leaves the reader absolutely convinced of the validity of your argument.

The most basic conclusion inverts the structure of the introduction, starting off with a restatement of the thesis statement, followed by more general statements that sum up the essay's main ideas. The final sentence is a broad remark about the subject or topic.

You can vary from this standard format in some instances. Many writers, for example, choose to introduce some new point or question in the conclusion that emerges from the thesis. After establishing the validity of the thesis statement, they then address its consequences or implications. Depending on the freedom your teacher allows, you might also try to be more creative in the conclusion. No matter the form of the conclusion, the same general rule applies: The conclusion should bring the essay to a formal close and affirm that the thesis statement has been proven.

Special Essay Types

There are many types of the essay your teachers may ask you to write. Besides the traditional five-paragraph format, you might have to write a persuasive essay, an expository paper, the personal statement, or a research paper. The following summaries familiarize you with the different focuses of each of these forms of writing.

The Persuasive Essay

A persuasive essay, also known as an argumentative essay, is just that: an essay that persuades the reader of some point or concept by proving and convincing the reader through your writing, examples, and citations that the concept is true. Think of a persuasive essay as a written way to get your reader to side with you and agree with what you are writing. Just as a lawyer argues his case to the jury, your writing will argue your idea and drive it home so that the reader comes away from it agreeing with you, or at least questioning what he may otherwise have believed.

Writing a persuasive essay requires you to use vocabulary and sentences that exude confidence in the point you are trying to make. Your word choice should be certain and strong, affirming and reaffirming your belief in your cause. Words such as: certainly, definitively, in fact, confidently, with conviction, and beyond a shadow of a doubt will help convince your reader of your commitment to your belief and main point you are proving.

Formatting your persuasive essay is similar to formatting the five-paragraph essay, where you use an introduction to introduce your argument followed by supporting paragraphs, and a conclusion. The difference? You want to add a paragraph that offers the opposing view of what you are trying to say. By doing this, you state the opposition and face it head on. By doing so, your reader recognizes your credibility even more since you are not afraid to face those skeptical of your argument. Be sure that you come back to your conclusion even more forcefully, however, driving your idea home and refuting why that opposition is still not as strong as your main argument.

Your essay should read like a well-organized conversation you are having with your reader, in a tone that is strong, accessible, yet confident. Each sentence should be written with conviction thereby setting a tone of certainty and confidence in your assertion or opinion.

Expository Writing

Like the five-paragraph and persuasive essay, expository essays consist of a thesis, supporting paragraphs, and a conclusion. What makes expository writing different is that it does not present your opinion or feelings about your topic. Rather it responds to a factual prompt (such as a question from history or science that explains an event or experiment) or request for basic information to be expressed (such as how to brush your teeth or program your DVR). Expository essays can also ask you to analyze or describe a process, idea, or event in time.

Expository essays are factual rather than based on opinion. They tend to make a point about something and often answer questions of "how" or "why" something has happened or is what it is. The essay does not offer the writer's point of view. It illuminates and analyzes matter-of-factly the views of others without debating or arguing a subject.

The Personal Statement

When writing a personal statement, you can basically throw out the window the rules of the five-paragraph essay. In terms of structure, tone, and concept, the personal statement is about *you*, written in the first person, and on a topic that only you could write about.

Personal statements are used often for college or graduate school applications to allow the admission office readers an opportunity to get to know you better.

Selecting a generic theme or topic is not a good idea for applications. Dig deeper to find stories that are meaningful and give the reader a glimpse of who you are. You will have an easier time piquing the interest of your reader and communicating your passion if you write about an experience, concept, conversation, challenge or life moment that is meaningful to you.

Here are some tips for writing a personal essay:

- You don't need to write about the most dramatic event of your life to separate yourself from the crowd. Good essays often stem from commonplace events.
- Feel free to use sentence fragments, pieces of dialogue or conversation, and humor if it suits you.
- Show more than you tell. Use examples instead of statements.
- Use your five senses when you write so your reader can see, hear, taste, smell, and feel your experience.
- Write in an authentic voice. Be open, honest, and always write in the first person.
- Practice reading your essay aloud or into a recorder. Does your essay sound like you? Is your voice coming through?

Be careful about seeking too much feedback from teachers, friends, or relatives. They can help you to determine if your voice is authentic, but they shouldn't be giving you ideas on what to write about.

The Research Paper

A research paper uses outside sources and a deep collection of your research to express information and support a particular point or topic. Research papers tend to be lengthier since they combine quotes from various sources as well as your thoughts and ideas about a particular subject.

ALERT

Plan to log many hours on the process of collecting, assimilating, distilling, and expressing the information you have gathered when you write a research paper.

Whatever the type of writing you are asked to do, be certain you understand from your teacher what is expected of you in terms of length, amount of research and outside sources necessary, and what sources you are expected to use outside of your own ideas. Also be certain to follow assignment guidelines. Some teachers want students to learn how to use the library system to do research, rather than doing all their research online.

QUOTE

"Whenever I get a writing assignment, I map out a plan on paper—kind of like an architect drawing plans—of the direction I want my writing to go, what supporting ideas, quotes, or facts I have to illustrate my point, and what conclusion I am trying to get my reader to believe. I view writing as kind of like creating a puzzle, completing the edges first, and filling it in with ideas that connect until it all makes sense and is complete."

—Beth C., Senior

CHAPTER 16

Revisions and the Final Draft

As you read and revise your first draft, try to think of yourself as an editor going over an article by a reporter. As an editor, it's your job to make certain that everyone will be able to understand the article. You might also try reading the essay out loud, to listen to how it sounds. At this stage, you need to worry about correct grammar and spelling, as they make it easier for the reader to understand and appreciate your ideas in the first place.

Reread Your Essay

Once you have completed the first draft, you should go back to the beginning and read it. Try to read it from an objective standpoint, as if you are someone else reading your work. Because you are so closely tied to your ideas, it will be difficult at first to be objective. As you read over the draft, ask yourself:

- Is everything explained fully?
- Will the reader understand everything as it is currently explained here?
- Are there any holes or gaps in the argument?
- Are any ideas not fully developed or partially explained?
- Does one idea flow smoothly into the next?
- What additional information does the reader need to appreciate my point?

Make appropriate notes. Try to anticipate questions a reader might have and write them in the margins. Now you're ready to rewrite. As you rewrite, answer the questions with more information. Revise the essay as many times as necessary, until you're satisfied with it. The changes you make will improve the essay with each draft.

The first few times you read and rewrite, you should focus on the content—the ideas and points that are explained in the essay. Make certain all your ideas are clearly and fully explained—that nothing is ambiguous or partially stated, that there are no gaps in the discussion. Examine the organization of the essay and make certain that one point flows smoothly and logically into the next. You might try moving sections of the essay around to see if they work more effectively somewhere else. Check that everything in the essay supports the thesis statement, and take out anything that detracts from the argument.

In later readings, you will concentrate more on the writing, grammar, and spelling. For now, review individual sentences and paragraphs to ensure the material is clear and flows together. Think about ways you can rework sentences to make them clearer.

When you are reviewing your essay, check to make certain you have met the page requirements set by your teacher. Remember, choosing the right topic from the start is the best way to ensure your essay will be the appropriate length. Once you've started writing, you may find your essay is a bit longer or shorter than you intended. If your essay is only half a page longer or shorter, most professors will still accept it. If it is off by more than half a page, then you need to make adjustments.

ESSENTIAL

The stages of writing: think, research, organize, draft, revise, edit, and proofread. Each time you revise, you make the essay a little better.

If you've included quotations and paraphrases from outside sources, you should also double-check the citations. Make certain you've given each source credit and followed the right format.

Turning in an essay that is not carefully edited makes a very poor impression on a teacher. It indicates that you don't take your work all that seriously. Even if the ideas within the essay are good, not taking the time to edit can lower your grade significantly. Make certain you review your essay carefully.

Proofread! Proofread! Proofread!

Always proofread your essay before turning it in. When you proofread, you are looking for errors specifically in grammar, spelling, and punctuation. It can often be difficult to catch them because, being accustomed to the essay as it stands, you simply do not see them. In order to proofread effectively, you need to read in a much more focused manner.

ALERT

If you feel comfortable, give your paper to a close friend, mentor, or teacher other than the one who assigned the paper to you. Sometimes fresh eyes can make you see things you missed or may not have considered. Conversely, beware that too many reviewers can take your voice out of the work you created. So pick and choose the feedback you receive and do not second-guess yourself or your instincts.

When you are ready, print out a clean copy of the essay. Bring your clean, printed-out copy to a location where there are absolutely no distractions. It is extremely important that the entire time you read, you keep foremost in your mind that you are trying to locate errors. If you forget this and get caught up in the content of the essay, you will continue to overlook mistakes. Read slowly and methodically, concentrating on each word and sentence. It is extremely helpful to read out loud, so that you can hear each word; you can also simply mouth the words silently. Hearing your words out loud also helps you identify where you may need extra commas, semicolons, or sentence breaks, too.

Your computer's spell-check program is helpful and can correct many errors, but it doesn't catch everything nor does it understand the misuse of a word. The spell-check will not catch homophones—words that sound the same but are spelled differently and have different meanings. You should always proofread yourself at least once after you've spell-checked your essay.

Sit with a dictionary in hand while proofreading, or keep an online dictionary site open on your computer. Get in the habit of looking up the definition of words you don't use frequently in conversation. In the process of writing and attempting to sound sophisticated, it is easy to use a word you think means one thing when it actually means something quite different.

Additionally, be aware of particular spelling or grammatical errors you are prone to make; whenever you get an essay back from a teacher, read it over to identify them. When you proofread, make certain you look specifically for those mistakes you tend to make.

Be certain you check the following elements in your final proofreading session. Be on the lookout for those mistakes you tend to make often.

- Spelling errors
- Mixed-up homophones
- Incorrect word usage
- Sentence fragments
- Run-on sentences
- Citation format
- Ambiguous references and pronouns (especially it, that, this, these, and those)
- Pronoun-antecedent agreement

Proofreading is a tedious process, but it is an important one. Remember, your writing is a reflection of you. A carefully proofread paper indicates a professional and serious attitude. And when the reader is your teacher, isn't that the impression you want to make?

Common Grammatical Errors

As important as your voice is in your writing and your thesis is in providing the central argument or message you aim to support throughout your essay, writing cannot be clear without using good grammar. Your ideas are the most vital part of any essay; without strong ideas, an essay will not be impressive, no matter how well written it might be. But correct grammar is also important—it is what makes your writing understandable and direct.

There are many different grammar rules. You can't possibly memorize them all, nor should you try. As a child you learned to speak without learning the "rules" of conversation by listening to others; you can also learn about grammar and language usage by reading. The more you read, the more you develop an "ear" for correct grammar. When you write, something will "sound" right or wrong to you. Try to read more frequently and trust your "ear" for correct grammar. If you have a serious problem with grammar, though, you may consider working with a peer or paid tutor.

Here is a list of some of the more common errors in grammar, punctuation, and language usage. These are errors you should particularly watch out for when you are proofreading your essay.

Homophones

Homophones are words that sound alike but have different spellings and meanings; they are extremely easy to confuse in your writing. Even when you proofread carefully, they can escape your attention and a computer's spell-checker often cannot distinguish between them. Watch out for homophones and make certain you have chosen the correct word.

These are some of the most commonly confused homophones:

- its/it's
- your/you're
- two/too/to
- there/their/they're
- whose/who's

Spelling Errors

Here's a list of frequently misspelled, commonly used words; you may even misspell them every time you use them without even realizing it.

absence	changeable	existence
accessible	commitment	exorcise
accommodate	committed	guarantee
acquaintance	conscience	half/halves
achieve	definitely	indefinitely
across	difference/different	independent
appearance	embarrass	indispensable
athlete	emphasize	insistent
bureaucracy	exaggerate	interpret
business	exercise	

judgment (or judgement)	perseverance	sophomore
knowledge	preference/preferred	succeed/successful
loneliness	prevalence	terrific
medicine	privilege	their
noticeable	pursue	tragedy
occasionally	refer/referred/referring	transfer/transferred
occur/occurred/ occurrence	repetition	undoubtedly
omit/omitted	rhythm	unnecessary
parallel	seize	vacuum
peace/peaceable	self/selves	worshipped
	separate	
	significance	

Most often, these words are misspelled because people get one or two letters wrong. Make certain you are familiar with these words so you can watch for them in your writing and double-check to see if they are correct.

Sentence Fragments

A sentence fragment is a group of words that does not function as a complete sentence. A complete sentence must consist of an independent clause—a group of words that includes a subject and verb and can stand on its own. The most common type of sentence fragment is one that lacks either a subject or verb. For example, "Justin's soccer game," or "Even though Ally had fun during her ballet class," are not complete sentences.

You can usually correct a fragment by adding a subject or verb, or by joining together separate fragments and remembering to add a comma.

Justin's soccer game lasted almost two hours.

Even though Ally had fun during her ballet class, she still had blisters on her toes.

When you proofread your essay, make certain each sentence has both a subject and a verb.

Run-On Sentences

Run-on sentences are the opposites of fragments. While a fragment does not contain an independent clause, a run-on sentence strings one clause or phrase after another, confusing the reader. A run-on is very confusing to read; you get lost somewhere in the middle of the sentence and forget what the whole thing is about. Most run-on sentences can be rewritten as two or three shorter sentences. Here is one that goes on and on:

Jacob continued to do math problems well into the night even when he felt too tired to do them he solved more and more and ate ice cream to keep himself awake and alert so that he could complete the entire assignment and also do the extra-credit question that the teacher required hoping that he could turn it all in on time.

As you can see, a run-on sentence is very confusing to read and the meaning gets jumbled around in your mind. Most run-on sentences can be rewritten in two or three shorter sentences, like this:

Jacob continued to do math problems well into the night. Even when he felt too tired to do them, he solved more and more. He ate ice cream to keep himself awake and alert so that he could complete the entire assignment and the required extra credit question. Jacob hoped that he could turn it all in on time.

Commonly Confused Expressions

The following list contains words or expressions that are frequently confused or misused. Most of them are homophones, words that sound the same but are spelled differently and have different meanings.

principle. A rule or law; a fact of nature.
principal. A person in authority, such as the head of a school. (Remember, the princi**pal** is your **pal**.)

capital. The seat of government (such as the city that is the state capital).
capitol. The building in which a governing body meets (as in the Capitol in Washington, D.C.).

affect. Used as a verb meaning to influence or to change. *The noise* affects *my ability to think.*

effect. Used as a noun, meaning the result of something. *The noise produces a negative* effect *on my work.*

stationary. Standing still.

stationery. Materials used for writing and typing. *The clerk was* stationary *behind the* stationery *counter.*

than. Used when comparing. *My chemistry book is heavier* than *my Spanish book.*

then. Used in reference to time; the next in order or time. *Let's go to lunch and* then *to the movies.*

your. A possessive; refers to something you own.

you're. A contraction of "you are." You're *going to be late to pick up* your *car.*

their. A possessive; refers to something they own. Their *house is red with white trim.*

there. Refers to location. *I left my car over* there.

they're. Short for "they are." They're *leaving in five minutes.*

its. A possessive; refers to what "it" owns.

it's. A contraction of "it is." It's *fun to watch the dog fetch* its *toys.*

quote. Used as a verb meaning to repeat something from another source.

quotation. Used as a noun meaning the reference that is repeated from another source. *He proceeded to* quote *from the passage, and the* quotation *was quite long.*

medium. A singular form of the word media referring to a single type of mass communication such as radio or television.

media. A plural form of the word medium that refers to several types of communication or to mass communication in general. *Television is a* medium *that is far more influential and important than the other* media.

Get to know the words on this list so you can watch out for them in your writing and double-check to make certain you use them correctly.

Pronoun-Antecedent Agreement

Pronouns (he, she, him, her, his, hers, their, theirs, it, its) take the place of nouns, and the nouns they refer to are called antecedents. Pronouns and antecedents must always agree, which means they must both be either singular or plural. For example:

Incorrect (Pronoun and antecedent do not agree)
  The students took his tests.

Correct (Pronoun and antecedent are both plural)
  The students took their tests.

There are two cases where this grammatical issue particularly becomes a problem: indefinite pronouns and generic nouns. An indefinite pronoun refers to a nonspecific person or thing, such as anybody, anyone, everybody, or someone. A generic noun represents a typical member of a group, such as a doctor, a student, or a New Yorker. Both of these antecedents are followed by *singular* pronouns: You should either use "he," "she," or "one" as the pronoun, or rewrite the sentence to avoid the problem.

Incorrect:
  When everyone has finished their exam, the test is over.
  A doctor must be considerate of their patients' feelings.

Correct:
  When everyone has finished his or her exam, the test is over.
  A doctor must be considerate of his or her patients' feelings.
  OR, Doctors must be considerate of their patients' feelings.

Dangling Modifiers

Modifiers are words or phrases that describe or elaborate upon some other word or phrase. Dangling modifiers do not logically refer to any word in the sentence and therefore make the sentence incoherent. Be particularly careful when a sentence begins with a modifier; whatever subject follows the modifier must be the one the modifier refers to:

Incorrect:
Originally performed in 1955, many people still consider Cat on a Hot Tin Roof to be Tennessee Williams's greatest play.

In the above sentence, the modifier "originally performed in 1955" refers to the play *Cat on a Hot Tin Roof,* and not the "many people." The sentence should therefore be rephrased:

Correct:
Originally performed in 1955, Cat on a Hot Tin Roof is still considered by many people to be Tennessee Williams's greatest play.

Split Infinitives

An infinitive form of a verb consists of two parts: the word "to" plus the verb. An infinitive is "split" when another word, usually an adverb, comes between them. Although certain constructions featuring split infinitives have come to be accepted, they generally sound awkward and disrupt the flow of a sentence. You should try to avoid them.
Split Infinitive:
My parents taught me to never chew with my mouth open.
Intact Infinitive:
My parents taught me never to chew with my mouth open.

Sentences Ending in Prepositions

Prepositions are certain words, usually appearing at the beginning of a phrase, that are used to describe or elaborate on some other word in the sentence. There are a limited number of prepositions in English. The most common include: about, above, across, after, against, along, among, around, as, at, before, behind, below, beside, between, but, by, concerning, despite, during, except, for, from, in, into, like, near, next, of, off, on, onto, out, over, regarding, respecting, since, than, through, throughout, to, toward, under, underneath, unlike, until, unto, up, upon, with, without.

It is generally considered poor grammar to end a sentence with a preposition. (Note though that this rule is changing and does not always apply today.) If a sentence ends with a preposition, try rephrase it if it does not sound even stranger, or try to place the preposition before the word it is modifying.

Incorrect:
> *What room is it in?*
> *Ross wanted to be read to.*

Correct:
> *Where is it?*
> *Ross wanted someone to read to him.*

Word Repetition

If you read an essay that uses the same words over and over, it can become quite boring and tedious. To make your writing more interesting for your reader, try to vary your choice of words as much as possible. You particularly want to use a sophisticated vocabulary that reflects your intelligence and expertise. To help increase word variety, you can use a thesaurus—a special dictionary of synonyms. You can buy a thesaurus in most bookstores to keep on your desk or use the one built into your computer.

When you edit your paper, look for any words that are repeated, especially within the same paragraph. Use the thesaurus to select alternatives. When using a thesaurus, you do need to be careful about which synonym you choose. Although synonyms have similar meanings, there are subtle differences that are important. Certain words are also more appropriate for a particular context. Additionally, some of the synonyms in the thesaurus might be old-fashioned words not frequently used. If you include them in your essay, these words will stand out and disrupt the flow of your argument. You should therefore only choose synonyms that you know and are comfortable using in your writing. If necessary, look up some of the suggested synonyms in a dictionary in order to see the exact definition and appropriate context.

One Last Look

Read your final version to make certain it is clean, neat, and correct. Correct any typos or other imperfections, and print it out again, if necessary. Include your name and the page number on each page, and staple the pages together. Either on the first page or on a title page, you should also include your name, the professor's name, the name of the course, and the title of your essay. The title should make the essay's topic very clear to the reader. You can, though, be a bit creative with the title to make the topic sound interesting and provocative. After you've completed editing, proofreading, and formatting the essay, print out the final version and turn it in!

QUOTE

"I have never considered myself to be a great writer—grammar, research, and sharing my thoughts through writing have never come easy. I am more of a math and science person, technical and precise. What I now realized, though, is that writing and especially grammar is extremely technical, kind of like a math puzzle, with rules, formats, and even solutions to try to achieve. When I view writing as a strategic exercise, it becomes easier for me to express myself within a structured context."

—Beth S., Junior

CHAPTER 17

Online Learning

In today's world of advanced technology, the four walls of a classroom and traditional brick-and-mortar school have expanded into a virtual world. Online learning, or e-learning, is a less traditional but more progressive way to obtain your education. Most colleges in the country now offer online courses, while others have entire programs that can be completed through e-learning.

Pros and Cons of Online Education

There are many advantages and disadvantages to e-learning. Consider your reaction to the pros and cons listed below to determine if this new and progressively growing type of learning is one you want to explore further.

Some of the advantages of e-learning include:

- Education is portable as long as you have access to the Internet and a computer. Just log on and you can be a student.
- You can work from virtually anywhere in the world, from a remote village to a rural farm region, as long as you can obtain Internet access.
- If you have a busy work or family life, you can do your class work at whatever time is convenient for you—morning, evening, or in the middle of the night (as long as you are not participating in an online chat discussion designated for a specific time!).
- If you move from one state to another or you or a spouse gets transferred for a job, you can't take your local state university with you, but your virtual university moves with you wherever you live.
- If you need to complete a few courses to graduate from college or want to take courses to supplement an internship or job experience you are having, e-learning is a more flexible and convenient alternative to attending a weekly, evening, weekend, or community-college class at a university near you.
- Online learning provides an alternate education opportunity for military families who are deployed and need to finish coursework or continue with classes while away from home. Military families who have to relocate can also benefit from this type of learning.
- In our uncertain economy, e-learning is a more affordable alternative, since the university doesn't have to host a class on campus with heating, lighting, a live professor, etc.
- Working moms, stay-at-home moms, or full-time working people can finish college or obtain advanced degrees, since online learning meets most needs of people living in our busy working world and varied society today.
- Students have the flexibility to take just a few e-courses to augment a college program, obtain a certificate in a field to advance a career, or earn an actual undergraduate, or graduate degree.

- Surprisingly, e-learning can actually be more personalized than sitting in a large college lecture hall. Most e-classes contain twenty-five to thirty students per course, and everyone gets a chance to think critically, give responses to the teacher, and obtain feedback from peers and professor. Course dialogue is created and you learn through it.

Here are some drawbacks to online education:

- E-learning does not provide many high school approved classes, and it's not currently designed to serve high school learners. Sometimes a few classes are offered online to serve as makeups for classes that students could not schedule into their class calendar or failed.
- Not all courses that may interest you are available through e-learning, although course catalogs at e-learning programs are growing daily.
- E-learning can't offer face-to-face learning, although Skype, iChat, social networking, and podcasts are being used more and more in this virtual world.
- E-learning cannot replicate a "real" on-campus college experience, including living and learning in a residential education system. It is limited to your computer connection.
- Internet access, if slow or unreliable, can prevent you from having a seamless e-learning experience. Be sure you feel confident with your computer skills and the reliability of your personal computer access or system.
- Computers crash, power goes out, batteries lose charge. Be sure your system is up and running and reliable.

Finding Reputable Online Schools and Classes

More and more schools are offering online learning programs or options. And having an online degree is gaining a better public perception and becoming more accepted. Online programs are also better regulated than they were a decade ago. To be accredited, they need to meet higher standards; schools are accountable and assessed for competencies and outcome-based results, and extensive followup is conducted on their graduates. New technologies, such as streaming video and podcasts, are being integrated into virtual classrooms to make classes feel more "real." Students can also offer feedback and take extensive surveys to evaluate their experiences with professors and courses.

Just as you do research to find a college or graduate program that suits you, be prepared to research your online education. Here are some tips:

- Look at the profiles and credentials of professors in the online university program. Make sure they are experts in their field.
- Seek out feedback through social networking with students who have participated in the program.
- Be sure that the online learning program has obtained university accreditations in approved specializations. If you're planning on pursuing a license in your field, make sure the program is nationally accredited. Do your homework in advance to be sure the classes you take, certificate you achieve, or degree you obtain will be accepted in your field as valid and accredited.
- Be sure the program is recognized by your state and that the university meets your own state requirements.
- Learn about graduation rates and job success of those who have completed a particular program.
- Visit websites such as www.ratemyprofessors.com that rate the university or professors you are considering. Or use social networking to visit college Facebook and Twitter pages that students generate.

Online Professor-Student Relationships

Just as you build teacher relationships through classroom participation, visiting during office hours, and being an active learner in traditional classroom learning, you need to get to know your virtual professor. Students can connect with professors via e-mail, Skype, iChat, classroom chat sessions, Facebook, or even podcast forums. Since there is a virtual distance between you and your professors and fellow students, you need to make connections through chats and your involvement in class. You need to actively make an effort to take the "distance" out of distance learning.

Online learning is a collaborative relationship in which the dialogue among faculty and learners and among individual learners becomes a thread that binds together virtual classrooms. Professor/student exchanges are both personal and academic. A good professor strives to facilitate critical thinking that is supported by the research and literature that are related to the assignment for the week.

How do you connect well with your teachers? E-learners need to ask questions, ask for feedback, and e-mail professors outside of class to be an engaged participant in her own learning process. Some e-learning programs offer a cyber café where learners chat with each other outside of class, as if in a coffee house. Sometimes courses also require real-time meetings in a chat format where you have a conversation once per week in real time with classmates and your professor via Skype, chat rooms, or iChat.

Some programs even conduct face-to-face graduation ceremonies, whereby all students assemble in one location to meet, graduate, and celebrate.

Formats of Online Classes

Since the evolution of e-learning continues to grow, there is not yet one "typical" way an e-student learns or receives information. Some classes are conducted via Skype or iChat, and all students have virtual face-to-face dialogue with their professors weekly regardless of their time zone or location. This is called a synchronous format of learning.

Other courses are formatted through chat rooms, online bulletin board postings, and text dialogues, and are known as asynchronous learning. For some classes, professors introduce themselves to students through a YouTube clip and then conduct a text- and e-mail-based course for the remainder of the term. In others, students never see a professor, but just "listen" through messages or postings.

Since one of the main benefits of online learning is being able to accommodate students' varied schedules, most schools use the asynchronous format. In some courses, though, students sign in once a week for a live chat format. Usually, you can see the professor's face and hear her voice, but the students reply through texting comments, questions, and conversation to a common board that everyone can read. The professor responds to the comments or questions orally or in a text message. Often, these synchronous sessions are not a required component for a grade, since many students in varied time zones or with career limitations would find participation in live chats difficult. Still, attend them if you can.

Some professors integrate video into their assignments or lectures. For example, in a counseling degree program, a professor may share a video clip of a counseling session and then ask students to partner up with an online classmate and create their own mock therapy session for the teacher to view. By interviewing each other, they get hands-on practice working as a therapist and are able to be critiqued by their professor when he views the uploaded clip.

Many professors who teach online are also professionals in their field of expertise. Online professional instructors have the benefit of bringing real-life examples into their virtual classrooms since they are out there daily doing their jobs that practically relate to their course.

ALERT

All professors online use turnitin.com, safeassign.com, or other sites that check submissions for plagiarism. Cite *everything* you find that is not your own work, both ideas and direct quotes or sources.

Weekly assignments and session questions are posted in a "course room" or assignment area online. Online courses, like brick-and-mortar classes, still use a syllabus and rubric for each course, which clearly presents course objectives and specific criteria that professors will use to evaluate their students. The rubric defines course expectations and breakdown of workload revealing more clearly how a student will be graded or evaluated by her professor. A rubric might look like this:

- Use proper APA or MLA format when writing or posting.
- Respond via post to at least two other comments from your classmates each day to contribute to ongoing classroom dialogue.
- Read postings daily from all of your classmates so you can keep up with course dialogue and uniquely contribute.
- Cite at least two quotations from your assigned class text and one idea you elaborate upon in your postings each week.
- Use 250 to 300 words per post.

Each student has a file that professors can access showing all the threaded dialogue a student wrote for the week. In this way, a teacher can scan the feeds to see how many students participate or how many times a student has properly posted. In the dialogue area, every student can view all of their other classmates' posts just as if they were speaking in the classroom. In a typical high school or college class, however, a student may get called on a few times per week, if at all. In contrast, online students are required to participate in classroom dialogue weekly for a specified amount of time, number of postings, or word count. This online dialogue allows students to think critically, evaluate, and express what they are learning. These dialogues also tell teachers which students are thinking originally and which are piggybacking off other classmates' ideas. Certainly there will be plenty of overlap when twenty-five students log in and comment on the same assignment or reading, but if the same students only repeat what others are texting before them, a professor may notice this weakness.

FACT

Online classes are usually small in size, about twenty to thirty students per class. Classes need to remain small to allow for the personalized dialogue to occur in this virtual setting. Online lecture classes do exist but are usually not participation-driven and more rote memory testing, multiple-choice, and papers are required as opposed to being graded on class participation.

Tests are given in secure locations online where students can upload an assigned paper or project. In some courses where rote memorization is required, a multiple-choice test can be administered securely, timed, and graded instantly online.

Web Etiquette for Students

Just as there are dos and don'ts in traditional classrooms, there are web etiquette standards in the e-learning community. Usually your school's website lists the rules of the virtual classroom and a code of ethics and honor they expect you to uphold and follow. Here are a few general web etiquette rules:

- Be respectful in your posts.
- Be respectful of diversity.
- Be truthful in your posted profile and photo.
- Follow the code of conduct described by your online school program. Often these rules will be posted and students have to sign off on them when they agree to take a course or enroll as a student at that online university.
- Read, be familiar with, and follow the rules of academic honesty that your online university uses.
- Be aware that you will be failed in a course if you plagiarize intentionally or unintentionally.

Treat your online community as if you were face to face with these classmates. If you wouldn't say something in public to a classroom of students then certainly do not feel you are safely hiding behind your computer screen. Be kind and respectful of your classmates.

Taking Online Tests

How tests are administered depends on the way each university handles them. Many tests are timed and standardized. You log in and your test is dated and time stamped; a timer is set online to count down how much time you have to complete a test. Online tests are proctored but are obviously all open-book tests. You need to prepare for the tests carefully and not assume they are easier just because you are taking them via computer. Tests are submitted online. In some cases, you can meet face to face with professors to take the test.

Tips for Success as a Distance Learner

To have a successful e-learning experience, you need to be involved in your education. You cannot sit back and wait for it to happen to you. Being well organized, good at time management, self-motivated, and willing to navigate this newer school system is crucial to your success. Take time to do online tutorials and orientations at your school to understand the learning platform that your particular school is using. Know how to perform what is expected of you in terms of online chats, posting your homework, and taking tests before you take a course.

All online universities employ special, sophisticated programs to check for plagiarism or improperly cited work. Professors can also Google strings of words to discover if they came from other sources. Entire papers can also be checked online against plagiarism search engines.

Also, twenty-four-hour tech support is offered at all of these e-learning programs so there can be no "the dog ate my homework" excuses or "it got lost through the e-mail." If your computer crashes, breaks down, or loses Internet connection call the tech support for help and create a paper trail of e-mails or live-chats so that you can protect yourself if your homework or test gets lost somehow.

"Learning online has literally revolutionized the way education can be obtained. As a stay-at-home mom, I am able to take classes in a non-traditional but cutting-edge way through a virtual classroom. My class-mates all connect with me online, and my professor is easier for me to reach than my teachers were on campus!"

—Jane R., Graduate Student

CHAPTER 18

Extracurricular Activities, Jobs, Volunteering, and Summer Plans

While the transcript is undeniably the most important component of your college application, being just a student is not your entire job. You need to find other activities to participate in outside of class that do not include watching TV, playing video games, or surfing the Internet. So, what can you do? Pick one activity and do it well. Or participate in a few activities but be sure you are doing more than just showing up. Join a club, sport, or organization and stick with it throughout school. Also, try to find time to get a job and volunteer as well during your time outside of school. Piece of cake, right?

Clubs, Athletics, and Organizations Are Important

Being a member of clubs, athletics, and organizations reflects another side of who you are. How you choose to spend your time outside of the classroom demonstrates what is important to you. Finding a few activities you enjoy doing (some people refer to that quality as being "well-rounded") or one main activity that permeates through all you do (referred to sometimes as a "pointy" student) offers your teachers, college admission officers, and others a glimpse into what else is important to you in your life. All colleges have activity sections in their applications that require you to complete lists, descriptions, and note hours dedicated to how you spent your time outside of class after school, on weekends, and during the summer. Make sure you have some items to add to that section!

Get Noticed: Be a Worker Bee

If you don't take on leadership responsibilities in a club, be a worker bee. Raise your hand and volunteer to do anything necessary to help in the club. Write e-mail blasts, distribute flyers, or man a booth at an event—anything. Do something other than just show up at weekly meetings. Plan to stay committed to an organization through your time in high school (unless you are totally miserable and it is a complete waste of time right off the bat). Stay committed for the long term and build up your role and involvement as a worker bee or eventual leader.

By getting more involved you will also have more to write about when it comes time to apply to colleges. Most colleges ask you to elaborate on an activity outside of school that excites you. A student who lists involvement in multiple clubs but cannot articulate anything tangible that she has done other than attend meetings is really not an effective or hands-on club member. Those students who demonstrate "depth and breadth" are viewed more favorably than those who simply attend weekly meetings. If it is not in your nature to lead, join and help out. Who knows? You may eventually become a club leader over time.

Starting Your Own Club or Organization

If you have an interest and your school does not have a club to support it, show some initiative and do it yourself. It is easier than you think! If you find yourself wanting to lead a club, take it on and go for it. Here's what you'll need to do:

1. Fill out an application form at school to get permission to start your club.
2. Put together your plans and a proposal, name your club, and define its purpose or mission.
3. Get a teacher to be the club advisor or supervisor and secure a location and regular meeting schedule.
4. Raise and designate uses for funds, plan events, bring speakers in to speak to your group, recruit members, and set goals.
5. Learn to promote through flyers, e-mail blasts, blogging, your school paper, or other campus outreach.
6. Learn to delegate tasks to members of the club and try to identify friends or classmates who can lead with you. Find underclassmen who will get involved so the club continues successfully even after you graduate.

Here are some ideas for off-the-beaten-path clubs:

- The MTV Club
- Cooking Club
- Pop Culture Club
- Scrabble Club
- Lawn Bowling Club
- Senior Citizen Support Club
- Hiking Club
- Classical Music Club
- Pet Owners Club
- Astronomy Club
- 4-H Club
- Harry Potter Club
- Star Wars Club

Get a Job

Wherever you live, whatever your family's income level, and no matter how much money your parents give you, sometime in high school and college you need to get a job. Being employed teaches you the real value of money and how much time and work it takes to make money.

Why Students Should Work

A job holds you accountable for being somewhere on time and answering to a supervisor other than your teachers or parents. Working also demonstrates to colleges and graduate schools that you are seeking out adult responsibilities and signifies a level of independence that you are creating for yourself. Having a job during high school, especially if you live in an affluent area, shows that you know what it is like to earn a dollar instead of taking handouts from your parents.

Don't rely on a job filing papers at your dad's office or answering phones at your mother's workplace. Instead, seek out "common jobs," such as bagging groceries, scooping ice cream, or making pizza. Babysitting is just fine, too. These types of jobs are ones you could easily get without your parent's help and also demonstrate initiative on your part.

FACT

Employers can also be good people to write college or graduate school supplemental recommendations for you. They can attest to your character in a different way than a teacher can, citing your work ethic, responsibilities, and demeanor at work.

If the time committed to working a job hinders your academic performance in any way, however, try to work only on the weekends or in the summer if possible. The *amount* of time you work is not as important as the fact that you *are* working. Find something that will build your character and perhaps introduce you to a world different from your own. Your brush with the working world will put things into clearer perspective for you. And, you'll never look at a five-dollar bill the same way again, once you realize what it takes to earn it! Also, going through the process of completing an application, interviewing with a supervisor or boss, and working out a shift schedule on your own is an adult experience. If the workload gets out of hand, try to hone your time management skills. Take ownership of your job experience in finding transportation (walk, bike, bus, drive, carpool) and being on time.

Ideas for Student Jobs

Coming up with jobs you can do in high school can be challenging since you may feel too young or inexperienced to work. Here are some good ideas for high school jobs:

- Ice cream scooper
- Coffee shop worker
- Water park or theme park ride attendant
- Grocery clerk or bagger
- Fast-food worker
- Landscaper or lawn mower
- Carwash attendant
- Babysitter
- Dog walker
- Retail stocker
- Shopping mall kiosk attendant
- Restaurant host or waiter

Here are some bad ideas for high school jobs: anything that looks as though you had your parents' help or connections in getting the job or can be viewed as though you are working for your parents, such as a law firm clerk, doctor's office file person, or other professional office gopher.

The Importance of Volunteering

While getting a paying job builds character and experience, so does giving your time away for free. Community service has become quite a buzz phrase in the college and graduate admission world, and admission officers do expect teens to have experience and awareness that comes from giving back to their communities. While many high schools have even implemented community service requirements to graduate, whatever your school does or does not require, volunteer anyway. And exceed the amount they do require if there is an expectation of you.

Choosing Meaningful Volunteer Work

The secret is this: volunteer work does not have to be a drag. Take something you already like to do and extend it into the area of community service. For example, if you like the beach, get certified and volunteer hours as a lifeguard or volunteer to organize a beach cleanup. If you enjoy drama, volunteer at an after-school Boys and Girls Club or community center and teach kids drama games and improvisation. Enjoy art or drawing? Recruit kids in your neighborhood to come do an "art class" with you each week. Organize a once-a-week volunteer craft project to help stay-at-home moms by entertaining their kids for a few hours of the day. Try to find something you like to do and link it to your community service. That way what can feel like a chore becomes fun.

QUESTION

How do I know if a volunteer job is the right one for me?
If you leave a volunteer job having enjoyed yourself, feeling good about what you did, and wanting to return again, it's right for you. Keep an open mind when it comes to trying new things.

Going Beyond the Minimum Hours

Many schools offer a minimum number of hours a student needs to complete in order to graduate. Use this number as just that: a minimum. In order to demonstrate that you weren't just volunteering to get your card signed off, go beyond the hours required by your school. If your school does not have a minimum or even a requirement, volunteer anyway. Not only does it feel good giving back, it is your duty to help those less fortunate in some way if you are blessed with good health, an education, and a life that affords you some luxuries.

Creating a Personal Volunteer Experience

Volunteer work can occur almost any way. Local hospitals, Boys and Girls Clubs, Special Olympics organizations, soup kitchens, schools, churches, shelters, libraries, and nonprofit organizations welcome students to assist in their organizations. Often it is as simple as completing an application and showing up during open hours. Working in hospitals or other medical settings may require fingerprinting or blood tests for infectious diseases so keep that in mind when applying.

ALERT

While joining a volunteer organization like National Charity League (NCL) can be a wonderful way to volunteer with your parent, you should in addition find something that is your "own" volunteer experience. NCL and other similar groups offer a variety of volunteer opportunities, but do something without your parent so that you can experience something more individualized and personally meaningful.

You get out of your volunteering experiences what you put in. That is, if you are passionate, open, committed, and excited to participate in your tasks assigned, the work will not feel like work and will give back to you in meaningful ways. Volunteering can take you into a world outside of your comfort zone, like a homeless shelter or soup kitchen, or it can serve as an extension of an existing talent or passion you have. For example, if you enjoy horses you can volunteer at a stable to clean stables or help children with disabilities learn to ride.

If you have an interest that does not have a volunteer organization linked to it, think about starting your own. If you like drama and theater, plan a summer camp or after-school drama class for youngsters in your own neighborhood. Make flyers, e-mail parents, give a presentation and start your own program. Or, if you are inspired by a book such as *Three Cups of Tea*, begin your school's volunteer club to raise awareness in Afghan schooling through the East Asia Institute.

VOLUNTEER DOS AND DON'TS

- **Do** volunteer to do something you enjoy and find meaningful.
- **Do** strive to make deep connections and commit yourself to the volunteer activity for an extended period of time to demonstrate depth of interest.
- **Do** seek out connections with the people you work with at your volunteer site, not only the recipients of your time, but your co-volunteers and volunteer coordinator.
- **Do** keep a personal log of hours you have committed to each organization.
- **Do** work hard as a volunteer since it can sometimes turn into a paid gig. Volunteer jobs may grow to something more permanent.
- **Do** work beyond the hours that are the minimum requirement of your school (if there is one) to demonstrate your longevity and sincere commitment to the organization.
- **Do** show up on time, ready to work, with respect and commitment.
- **Don't** volunteer somewhere simply because you think it "looks good" for college or graduate school.
- **Don't** disparage or speak down about your co-volunteers, the organization, or people you serve.
- **Don't** treat a volunteer job as unimportant just because you are not being paid for your time.

Overall, volunteering should not be a drag; it should be fun and rewarding. You should look forward to doing it since you will be helping others or an organization by giving of your time, mind, and self.

Spend Your Summers Wisely

As soon as you graduate from eighth grade, in the eyes of colleges you are a high school student. That means that beginning the summer after eighth grade, your summers "count." Does that mean you can't hang out, relax a bit, and decompress after a busy year in school? No. It just means you do need to plan some activities for yourself to keep your summers filled and active through high school and college. Going to the beach, playing video games, hanging out at the mall, and watching television are not great answers to fill in on the college application question: How did you spend your high school summers?

Certainly you can go on a family trip or two, unwind, and hang out. But be sure to fill the remaining time with some significant experiences. Whether it be attending summer school, working at a coffee bar, learning a musical instrument or new language, or some other activity, make sure to take advantage of the extra free time you have in the summer and use your time wisely.

Check out *www.tipsontripsandcamps.com* for a terrific resource of prescreened programs that have been endorsed and approved by real kids. The site uses an extensive questionnaire and feedback process from actual students who have attended the programs so you know what you are getting into has been successful for others already.

Begin to think about your upcoming summer in January of that year so you can look into application requirements to certain activities or programs. Sometimes teacher recommendation letters are required when you apply so plan ahead (remember those all-important teacher relationships!). Here are some areas to consider when planning your summer.

The Academic Summer

Participate in summer school courses or programs on college campuses—either close to home or far away. You do not need to find a college where you would necessarily want to apply; any campus is fine. See if the program offers college credit or high school credit as a result of your program. Obtain an official transcript and have one sent to your high school counselor as well when the program is complete.

Explore a subject that interests you in greater depth. For instance, if you like English literature, take a course on William Shakespeare. Or, alternatively, try exploring an interest you have never cultivated but want to learn more about such as a new language, film, music, anthropology, architecture, or forensics to name a few.

Virtually all college campuses offer summer programs for high school students or current college students. If you want to obtain credit, you need to see that course will be transferable to another university. If credit does not matter and you want to just learn for learning's sake, take a course with a pass/fail or credit/no credit option. Or audit a class so that you can just enjoy listening and learning but do not have to stress about being tested or writing papers for the class.

ESSENTIAL

If you travel with family or friends in the summer, try to find ways to make your trips educational and even academic. Read books about the history of the place you are visiting and go to museums and historic sites.

Studying Abroad

There are a plethora of summer opportunities available to students all over the world. You can work on your language skills, learn a new language in an immersion program, or just embrace a culture other than your own for the summer. Some students want to live with a family in another country, to gain an insight into another culture firsthand. Others prefer living in a dormitory environment with other students from around the country. There are pros and cons to both experiences.

National organizations support overseas experiences, such as People to People Sports Ambassadors (Eisenhower), Lead America, or American Field Service (AFS). Also, many college campuses have relationships with universities overseas whereby you can gain transferable college credit by studying at those institutions. Check with your school before you go to be sure coursework you pursue will be transferable if you need it to be.

Summer Community Service

Spend your summer giving back in a significant way. Programs around the globe offer you the opportunity to make a difference in the world by giving your time to help build houses, schools, or give back to communities much less fortunate than your own. Find out what your local church or religious organization has planned for the summer in volunteer outreach and sign up.

If you like the beach, by all means go there and enjoy it, but consider getting a job as a lifeguard, at the snack bar, or organize a beach cleanup so you can do some community service while there, too. Find things you enjoy and brainstorm ways you can delve deeper into your passion in the summer months and capitalize on the free time you have when you are out of school.

Summer Athletic Programs

Certainly your sport will require you to do some training or camps over the summer. If you are a varsity athlete, you will probably be required to practice or play in a summer league, which certainly makes it harder to find time for other organized programs. Colleges do recognize the severe time commitment involved in sports. If you can, pursue a new athletic endeavor or some extra sports-related activities such as coaching, working as a referee, or teaching at a community center or summer camp sports program.

College campuses offer a variety of organized sports programs in the summer under the guidance of college athletes and coaches. If you are in college, you can work or volunteer as a coach, and if you are in high school you can enjoy learning from excellent college athletes and coaches.

Summer club sports teams also play and practice as well as compete in tournaments around the country and sometimes internationally. Furthermore, there are showcases that high school athletes also attend in summers where college scouts look to recruit.

Leadership Programs

Seek out leadership programs that teach you fundamentals of leadership through group and team-building activities. You will attain skills such as public speaking, working in teams, and oftentimes hear presentations from local leaders in your area on how they achieved their goals and the skills they used to become an effective leader.

Fine Arts or Performing Arts Programs

Are you a dancer? Singer? Musician? Artist? Actor? Seek out a program that allows you to hone your craft. Again, college campuses, conservatories, local theaters and repertories, and high schools offer classes to learn acting, technical aspects of theater, etc.

ESSENTIAL

Be creative. Do you love airplanes? Then take some simulated flying lessons, volunteer at an airplane museum, or try to take a behind-the-scenes tour of your local airport to educate you on how things work. Like to cook? Sign up for some classes at a nearby culinary institute or try to intern for a chef at any local restaurant. The sky's the limit.

Outdoor Adventure and Travel Opportunities

Do you dare climb a mountain? Get close to nature? Push yourself to limits you never thought imaginable? Live and survive in the great outdoors? Try some adventurous travel.

QUOTE

"I worked at my local grocery store as a bagboy. The pay was okay and I got a free Subway sandwich with every shift. I learned a lot about people by being a bagboy, how they treat others, who is grumpy or friendly, and also about customer service. I also learned responsibility, how to save money since now it means much more since I earn it myself. My parents still pay for my gas but I am now in charge of movies, pizza on the weekends with friends, and any recreation I do with them. Twenty dollars sure runs out fast!"

—Mike F., Sophomore

CHAPTER 19

Find and Pursue Your Passion

Through your years of schooling, you gain exposure to a variety of subjects, teachers, and extracurricular activities. During the course of your job as a student, you may have discovered those classes or activities that make you most excited: your heart skips a beat when thinking about it, you arrive in class more enthused for this subject, and overall you are discovering your passion. Find something you like to do and thread it through your high school experience. Consider the suggestions in this chapter and apply this thought process to your passion.

The Focused Student

Focused students usually have one specific passion or academic category that excites them the most. Below is a description of a student type followed by quotes from actual students in each category. Try to find some of yourself in any or many of the below listed categories of students.

The Academic

Are you an academic? If you love reading and English (or any particular discipline more than most), be sure you are reading outside of the classroom, attending book signings at local store events or even starting or participating in you school's own literary club. Why not try to enter some writing contests and get published? Or see if your teacher or a local college professor would like help with her research or as a teaching assistant.

> Real student experience: "As a rising high school senior, I was excited to take the AP Art History class offered only to seniors. When I signed up for classes late in my junior year, to my disappointment the course was not being offered. I went to the art teacher and asked why, to which she replied, "There are not enough students interested so the administration decided not to offer it."
>
> "How many students do they need?" I inquired.
>
> "At least eight," my teacher replied.
>
> And so I was off. Mind you, this was before the days of e-mail and text messaging. I got on the telephone that night and called as many classmates as I knew to convince them to sign up. I went around tables at lunchtime promoting the class and even at recess or breaks between class, and encouraged my classmates to sign up. "It is a great AP, guys. Plus we get to sit in the dark and look at slides of art and talk all about it. And we may even earn college credit for it," I urged.
>
> By the end of the week I had twelve students sign up (not an easy feat for a class that totaled eighty-eight students). AP Art History was back

to being offered. P.S. All of us earned a three, four, or five on the AP exam to boot! And, later I wrote about that experience in my college applications as an example of leadership and "intellectual vitality." At the time I wasn't thinking of how this story would impact my college applications, but I believe in some small way it did demonstrate my character.

Take your high school experience into your own hands. You *do* have some control over things in the realm of your education, even if you think you do not.

The Actor

Have you always been interested in theater? Do you enjoy performing? How about attending theater? Do you ever volunteer your time as an usher at a local theater or helping at the local elementary school play? How about learning more about behind-the-scenes stage work such as costumes, lighting, or set design? Why not look into a summer theater program for high school students?

Real student experience: One summer I applied to a summer theater institute for high school students. I lived on a college campus and experienced life away from home, in a dormitory. Doing laundry wasn't easy! It was the most defining and best extracurricular experience I had had in my life up to that point. Later, I went on to write my college essay/personal statement about an aspect of that summer.

Seek out opportunities outside of school to enhance your interests and stretch yourself as a person.

The Athlete

Are you athletic? Do you spend time playing your sport in the summers? Helping coach the sport to youngsters or those less fortunate? Have you ever organized a club related to your sport or a fundraiser for your team? Do you attend professional or college level sports events that can teach you more about your sport when you act as an observer?

Real student experience: I had participated in summer sports camps for many years but wanted something more. Volunteer coaching was a great way for me to appreciate my sport by educating me about my sport from a new vantage point.

The Chef

Do you enjoy cooking as a hobby? Do you like to experiment in the kitchen or with ingredients in your mom's pantry? Ever thought about collecting recipes from your classmates and putting together a "Best of Your High School" cookbook? You could donate the proceeds to send someone who cannot afford it to attend a cooking school. Ever tried to hone your cooking skills by volunteering at a local restaurant or by taking classes at a culinary institute or Sur La Table or Williams Sonoma store?

Real student experience: As a male athlete I thought maybe cooking was a strange interest for me. But I loved it so I signed up for some cooking classes on the weekends at a local community center. Before I knew it I could julienne, braise, and make mire-poix. (Look that one up!) Learning cooking academically made me more comfortable experimenting in my home kitchen, so now every Friday night my mom grocery shops and I make our family meal.

The Obscure Hobby Enthusiast

Have an unusual passion for something quirky such as Scrabble or an activity like knitting or collecting coins?

Real student experience: I rediscovered my love for Etch-a-Sketch on a long bus ride home from a soccer game against a rival high school. My friend had a mini-keychain Etch-a-Sketch looped onto his backpack and I was bored so I asked him if I could play with it. I enjoyed it so much and was actually pretty artistically talented. My love of drafting— I wanted to be an architect—was put to good use on that little screen. At home I dug up my old Etch-a-Sketch toy from childhood at the bot-

tom of my closet and eventually became addicted. No joke, I actually formed my school's first ever Etch-a-Sketch Club. Once a week, students of all grades were invited to meet in a courtyard, Etch-a-Sketches in hand, and turn those white knobs to create whatever entered his/her imagination. By the end of recess we shared our work and shook our creations goodbye. We even organized a school fundraiser once and donated our proceeds to purchase dozens of Etch-a-Sketches for a Toys for Tots holiday drive.

The Well-Rounded Student

Well-rounded students often have multiple passions or seem to like too many things and cannot just choose one to thread through their academic or extracurricular experience. Colleges and universities admit both focused and well-rounded students so one type is not preferred as an applicant to another.

Find some things you like to do and connect them in your high school years in a way that makes sense to you both in terms of a time commitment and your level of enthusiasm for the activity. You don't need to be one-dimensional and too focused on one theme throughout your high school years; rather, pursue extra experiences to supplement, enhance, or further educate or expose you to your passion. You can love something more deeply and still be "well-rounded."

Aptitude and Personality Tests

What if you have not yet identified your passion? If you have not discovered your goals in life and feel either lost or overwhelmed by the thought of selecting a major or pursuing a career path, you may be a great candidate for finding some answers and direction by taking an aptitude or personality test. The best known of these multiple-choice tests is the Myers-Briggs Type Indicator (MBTI), which offers a series of pointed questions. The answers are not based on right and wrong, but instead indicate to the analyzer where your potential career and personal interests lie. How you respond to each question helps determine your personal strengths and possible career or academic interests, and may assist you in finding a career path or college major that is right for you.

FACT

There are other ways to take personality tests that are less formal than the MBTI. Search online for some reputable personality tests you can take to help identify skills and passions you have that can be linked to college majors, internships, or careers.

Professional career or guidance counselors are trained to assist you in finding a path and direction to take to pursue your career or academic aspirations. Many schools have in-house guidance counselors or advisors, but you can seek out an independent professional if you need a more in-depth study of what direction you might pursue. These professionals will interview you and use your verbal responses to help formulate and identify majors or career paths that would be a good fit for your personality type and interests.

Be an Educational Consumer

When you're a student, especially at a big school, it's easy to feel like a small part of a very large system. As you plow through miles of red tape and deal with headache-inducing bureaucracy, you can feel you have no control over your education and that your only option is to do what you are told.

Don't forget, though, that without students, there wouldn't be an education system. You are a vital part of any educational institution and, as such, you have a right to make as many demands on the system as it makes on you. Your education is at stake, and you have the right to get the best one possible—especially since you are paying for it.

If you read consumer magazines and advice guides, you'll see references to becoming an educated consumer. This means that before you make a major purchase, you do some research to get the best buy. You should similarly become an educated consumer of education. Get your money's worth from your school.

Being an educated consumer starts first with choosing a school that's right for you. There are more than 3,500 colleges and universities out there, but only a handful are going to suit your interests and needs. Don't choose a school haphazardly based on what other people tell you or where you think you should go.

ESSENTIAL

Visit Facebook or college blog posts to hear directly from current students what is on their minds. Also read different campus student newspapers online to get a better sense of the culture and flavor of the student body.

Do some research. Most schools are different than the glossy promotional brochures make them out to be. It's a good idea to visit them in person so you can see how things really are. The administrators and admissions officers will give you one point of view about a school, but students may tell you something else. Try to talk to students and ask about their perspectives. Do they like the school? Do they feel they are getting a good education? Are they happy with the choice they made?

Look carefully at recent statistics about the school. How many people drop out before graduating? How long does it take most students to get a degree? What percentage go on to find jobs within a year of graduating? What percentage of students continue on to graduate or professional schools? If these statistics are poor, the school may not provide its students with everything it should.

FACT

Visit colleges. Take time to tour college campuses, whether they are schools you will apply to or not. It is important to see what your goal is in doing this "job" called high school. Any time you are traveling near a college campus, even if it is close to home, take a tour, visit the bookstore, and ask current students lots of questions to get a feel for the campus culture. Don't be shy!

Once you are attending a school, you should continue to think of yourself as an educated consumer. Most schools have a tremendous range of offerings; there are many different courses as well as many different teachers. Both teachers and courses, though, can range in quality. It would really be a shame to spend money for college credits and end up in courses that do not excite or appeal to you. Sometimes a course won't be good because its content isn't something that interests you. More often than not, though, the deciding factor is the professor. A dynamic teacher can make the most mundane of subjects seem interesting. A poor teacher, however, can make the most fascinating subject matter a total bore. Before you select classes, do some research to be sure you'll get what you want.

Where Will You Go?

There are many different sources of information you can consult about which college is best for you. Because the following sources do not all provide the same kind of information, you should consult several of them. The more information you have, the more well-rounded the picture of the school you're researching will be.

College Guides

There are almost as many college guides on the market as there are colleges. Many guides simply list basic facts about the schools, such as the number of students, the student-to-teacher ratio, requirements to graduate, majors offered, and average SAT scores of those admitted; other guides are more subjective, trying to paint a portrait of life at the school and to elaborate on each school's strengths and weaknesses. Both kinds of books can be quite valuable, particularly in the early stages of your college search when you are identifying a range of schools that are right for you. As you narrow down your choices, you can get more detailed information from other sources.

Websites

All colleges and universities have their own websites. Visit these sites and get a variety of information about a school. Check out online course catalogs, campus clubs and organizations, school traditions, and the student online newspaper, seeking any particular areas of interest to you. Your goal is to try to get a feel of the vibe of a campus without having visited. So dig deep and read student testimonials and anything that will give you the flavor and feel of a campus. There are also several online college guides, many provided by the same publishers as the college guide books you see in the bookstore.

College Brochures and Catalogs

You can write or e-mail specific schools and request information. Keep in mind that their brochures are designed to present the school in the best possible light. Essentially school-produced booklets and publications are public relations pieces and advertisements. Still, the brochure will provide important basic information. Additionally, peruse the online course catalog.

Friends and Relatives

Ask people where they went to school (or are currently going) and how they feel about it. Ask specific questions about assets and drawbacks. Keep in mind, though, that people are different. What one person may have loved or hated about the school may not affect you the same way. Be wary especially of the "Legacy Trap"—just because a close relative went to a particular school and loved it does not mean it's necessarily the best place for you. Consider your own interests and needs, and find a school that meets them.

Campus Visits

Visiting a school is an excellent way to get a tremendous amount of information about it. You'll see the campus the way it really looks, not as it appears in the fancy brochure photos. Go on a campus tour and check out the admissions office, where there is often some kind of information session for students. Make certain you talk to students; they will give you an accurate assessment of the school from the student's point of view. If possible, arrange to stay overnight in a dormitory (most schools make this experience available to applicants). Of course, visiting schools is time-consuming and can be expensive; you should plan to visit only those schools you are seriously considering attending.

ESSENTIAL

Keep a notebook to log your campus visits. Note cool facts, traditions, campus tour highlights, e-mail addresses of currents students you may have met, and names of special classes or professors you may have collected. You will refer back to these notes when it comes time to apply to college and even may use some of the content you gathered in your actual college application questions.

Making the Most of School

Throughout this book you have learned that it is important to be an active rather than a passive student. That not only applies to your specific study tasks, but to your entire attitude as a student. You can't sit back and place your education entirely in the hands of others. Teachers, books, and other educational resources can only do so much; ultimately, you must take control of your own education if it is going to have any value. In part, this means getting help when you need it. There are many resources available to help you when you are having difficulty, including caring teachers and tutoring programs, but you've got to make the effort to seek them out.

At the same time, you can supplement your education on your own. Schools today are rich in resources and opportunities that can provide you with an exceptional, well-rounded education, from study-abroad programs and career internships to high-tech study centers and libraries. But these opportunities are not going to come knocking on your door; you need to take active measures to find and use them. If you make the most of your education, it will eventually mean much more to you than a diploma hanging on the wall. It will mean you have done a successful job in charting your path towards a future that you created. The foundation your education provides is more sturdy and stable if you have taken an active role in crafting and working at it.

In the meantime, good luck and happy studying.

FINAL IMPORTANT POINTS TO REMEMBER

- Develop productive study habits and make them a part of your daily routine. Change bad habits into good ones.
- Treat being a student like a job; be professional, serious, and organized.
- Set tasks for each day, week, and month.
- Manage your time carefully; create a schedule that gives you flexibility each week to fulfill new tasks.
- Make the right impression on your teacher. Take pride in your work.
- Be an educated consumer.
- Take control over your education and make the most of it.

QUOTE

"Dance is my thing so I do it whenever and wherever I can. I subscribe to dance magazines, read professional dancers' blogs, teach dance to underprivileged kids, compete on my school dance team, and dance around my kitchen and living room while preparing dinner. Dance is my life outside and inside of high school and everyone knows it. Why not always do something you love?"

—Theresa M., Sophomore

APPENDIX A

Study Calendar

Sunday

Time	Activity
8–9:00	
9–10:00	
10–11:00	
11–12:00	
12–1:00	
1–2:00	
2–3:00	
3–4:00	
4–5:00	
5–6:00	
6–7:00	
7–8:00	
8–9:00	
9–10:00	

Monday

Time	Activity
8–9:00	
9–10:00	
10–11:00	
11–12:00	
12–1:00	
1–2:00	
2–3:00	
3–4:00	
4–5:00	
5–6:00	
6–7:00	
7–8:00	
8–9:00	
9–10:00	

Tuesday

Time	Activity
8–9:00	
9–10:00	
10–11:00	
11–12:00	
12–1:00	
1–2:00	
2–3:00	
3–4:00	
4–5:00	
5–6:00	
6–7:00	
7–8:00	
8–9:00	
9–10:00	

Wednesday

Time	Activity
8–9:00	
9–10:00	
10–11:00	
11–12:00	
12–1:00	
1–2:00	
2–3:00	
3–4:00	
4–5:00	
5–6:00	
6–7:00	
7–8:00	
8–9:00	
9–10:00	

Thursday

Time	Activity
8–9:00	
9–10:00	
10–11:00	
11–12:00	
12–1:00	
1–2:00	
2–3:00	
3–4:00	
4–5:00	
5–6:00	
6–7:00	
7–8:00	
8–9:00	
9–10:00	

Friday

Time	Activity
8–9:00	
9–10:00	
10–11:00	
11–12:00	
12–1:00	
1–2:00	
2–3:00	
3–4:00	
4–5:00	
5–6:00	
6–7:00	
7–8:00	
8–9:00	
9–10:00	

Saturday

Time	Activity
8–9:00	
9–10:00	
10–11:00	
11–12:00	
12–1:00	
1–2:00	
2–3:00	
3–4:00	
4–5:00	
5–6:00	
6–7:00	
7–8:00	
8–9:00	
9–10:00	

Standardized Testing

Whether getting your driver's license or taking the SATs, each test you take is a rite of passage that you'll have to go through when you reach a certain age or experience level. There are proactive ways you can plan and tutoring available to assist you if you feel overwhelmed or in need of extra support and guidance as you navigate these types of tests.

Types of Standardized Tests

There are many types of standardized tests that you will be required to take during your high school and college years. Most colleges require that applicants submit results from one or more standardized test as part of the admission process. Most all colleges will now accept *either* the results from the SAT Reasoning Test (formerly the Scholastic Aptitude Test or the Scholastic Assessment Test) *or* the ACT (American College Test) both of which include a writing section. Additionally, some colleges, including the University of California and many highly selective universities, require some combination of SAT II subject tests.

Your high school may have internal or state mandated standardized tests such as the STAR testing or Stanford 9 test. Some private schools use certain tests to measure the student body, and public schools have other standardized test measures. Below, however, are definitions of the national tests used in the college admission process followed by the college-level testing required for graduate school admissions. These are just general overviews simply to familiarize you with the names of the various testing agencies.

PSAT and PLAN Tests

The PSAT (Preliminary SAT) is similar to the SAT Reasoning Test and shorter in length, usually administered by schools in tenth grade. The test is not always a great indicator of how you will do on the real SAT, though. The PSAT is also known as the NMSQT (National Merit Scholar Qualifying Test), which identifies National Merit Scholars based on the scores they receive on this test. The PSAT is not required for college admission and scores are not reported to colleges. It doesn't hurt to take it as it is good preparation for the SAT, though.

The PLAN (National Assessment Program for Literacy and Numeracy) test is the prequel to the ACT test. PLAN is taken in tenth grade. A test called EXPLORE is taken in eighth or ninth grade and is the pre-PLAN standardized test. All are owned by ACT.

SAT Reasoning Test

The SAT Reasoning Test is a three-hour, primarily multiple-choice test that measures verbal and mathematical reasoning abilities that develop over time. There is an essay writing section as well. The test scale goes to 800 with a math, verbal, and Essay component. The total possible perfect score a student could achieve would be 2400 points. The SAT Reasoning Test and SAT II subject tests are products owned by the College Board. Visit *www .collegeboard.com* for additional information.

ACT

The American College Test (ACT) tests students in fours areas: English, mathematics, reading, and science reasoning. There is also an ACT Plus Writing test that has the previous four sections plus a thirty-minute writing section. Check to see if your colleges require the writing test; most these days do. Also most colleges will accept results of the ACT as an alternative to the SAT I, and, in some cases, the SAT II subject tests. From the ACT.org website: "ACT results are accepted by all 4-year colleges and universities in the U.S. The ACT includes 215 multiple-choice questions and takes approximately 3 hours and 30 minutes to complete, including a short break (or just over four hours if you are taking the ACT Plus Writing). Actual testing time is two hours and fifty-five minutes plus thirty for the writing section (ACT Plus Writing)." The test is scored on a scale of one to thirty-six.

Advanced Placement Tests

Advanced Placement (AP) Exams are graded on a scale one to five. They are usually taken in May or June or after the completion of a specific AP course. Usually a score of four or five will earn a student college level credit at universities, although that varies from school to school. A score of three will often assist with college placement in more advanced-level college classes (e.g., foreign language placement, English, etc.) than if you received a two or one or no AP credits.

SAT Subject Tests

The SAT Subject Tests (formerly SAT2) are one-hour, multiple-choice tests that measure a student's knowledge of particular subjects and the ability to apply that knowledge. A generation ago they were known as Achievement Tests. The scale is the same range as SATs of 200–800. SAT Subject Test scores assist colleges with placement level of students in various courses. They measure how a student's school does in teaching subject material and how good a multiple-choice test taker the student is. Students can take up to three subject tests in one day since each test is multiple-choice and an hour in length. SAT Subject Tests should ideally be taken just after a particular course is completed. (Visit Collegeboard.com for a complete listing of subjects offered and current testing dates.)

Which Tests Should You Take?

Students usually register to take either the SAT Reasoning Test and/or the ACT with writing supplement in the spring of junior year. (Some choose to take it the fall of senior year since they feel less busy and overwhelmed by school-year commitments and prepare the summer leading up to the test date.) The option of taking either the SAT Reasoning Test or the ACT is mentioned because colleges which accept both tests use a "conversion chart" to compare a student's score on either the SAT Reasoning Test or the ACT. The higher score is used for admission purposes. In fact, some colleges will actually use the best combination of scores from various sittings of the tests in making an admission decision. There are even over 800 colleges today that have made the SAT or ACT optional or not required for admission. You can see a list of these schools at *www.fairtest.org*.

All SAT Subject Tests should be taken as soon as you can after your completion of the course, so ideally in May or June (unless it is a one-semester class). At the same time you may already be studying for that subject for your exams or AP testing so the material is no different. Check to see which math level your college will accept. Many do not count the Math Level 1C, for example.

On each test day, a student can take either the SAT Reasoning Test only *or* up to three SAT Subject Tests. Ideally, testing should be completed by

December of your senior year or sooner if you plan to apply to some colleges earlier, under Early Decision (ED) or Early Action (EA) application deadlines.

Preparing for Standardized Tests

A good starting point is to read through the online sites and registration and sample test booklets provided by the SAT and the ACT, which are available at your college counseling center at your school. Also, practice tests are offered on the websites. Test prep books are sold at all bookstores and online as well.

A multitude of tutoring companies offer preparation courses to familiarize you with the contents and assist in preparatory planning. The best preparation is to actually take practice tests. Scores often improve dramatically because you have learned by experience how to take the test.

APPENDIX C

Resources and Websites

High School

Gottesman, Greg. *College Survival: Get the Real Scoop on College Life from Students Across the Country.* (New York, NY: Peterson's, 2004).

Gottesman, Greg. *High School Survival: A Crash Course for Students by Students.* (New York, NY: Arco Books, 1999).

Riera, Michael. *Surviving High School.* (Berkeley, CA: Celestial Arts, 1997).

The Admissions Process

Fetter, Jean. *Questions and Admissions: Reflections on 100,000 Admissions Decisions at Stanford.* (Stanford, CA: Stanford University Press, 1995).

Rubenstone, Sally. *College Admissions: A Crash Course for Panicked Parents.* (New York, NY: ARCO, 1994).

Springer, Sally, Jon Reider, and Marion Franck. *Admission Matters.* (San Francisco, CA: Jossey-Bass, 2009).

Steinberg, Jacques. *The Gatekeepers.* (New York, NY: Penguin Books, 2003).

Thacker, Lloyd (editor). *Colleges Unranked.* (Portland, OR: The Education Conservancy, 2004). Essays by professionals in college counseling.

Van Bursick, Peter. *Winning the College Admission Game: Strategies for Students and Parents.* (Lawrenceville, NJ: Peterson's, 2007).

Competitive Colleges

Antonoff, Steven. *The College Finder.* (New York, NY: The Ballantine Publishing Group, 1999)

Fiske, Edward B., *The Fiske Guide to Colleges.* (Naperville, IL: Sourcebooks Inc., annually updated.)

Greene, Howard and Matthew Greene. *The Hidden Ivies: Thirty Colleges of Excellence.* (New York, NY: Cliff Street Books, 2000).

Montauk, Richard and Krista Klein. *How to Get Into the Top Colleges.* (New York, NY: Prentice Hall, 2000)

Alternative Colleges

Mathews, Jay. *Harvard Schmarvard: Getting Beyond the Ivy League to the College That Is Best for You.* (New York, NY: Three Rivers Press, 2003).

Pope, Loren. *Colleges That Change Lives: 40 Colleges You Should Know About Even If You're Not a Straight-A Student.* (New York, NY: Penguin Books, 2000).

Pope, Loren. *Looking Beyond the Ivy League: Finding the College That Is Right for You.* (New York, NY: Penguin Books, 1995).

College Visits

Spencer, Janet and Sandra Maleson. *Visiting College Campuses.* (New York, NY: Princeton Review Publishing, 2004).

The Essay

Muchnick, Cynthia and Mark Stewart. *The Best College Admission Essays.* (New York, NY: Peterson's, 2004).

Summers and Scholarships

Peterson's *Summer Opportunities for Kids and Teens.* (New York, NY: Thomson Peterson's, 2005).

Peterson's *Summer Study Abroad.* (New York, NY: Thomson Peterson's, 2005).

Peterson's *Scholarship Grants and Prizes.* (New York, NY: Thomson Peterson's, 2005).

Schwebel, Sara. *Yale Daily News Guide to Summer Programs.* (New York, NY: Simon & Schuster, 2004).

Financial Aid

The College Board. *Getting Financial Aid.* (New York, NY: The College Board, updated annually).

O'Shaunessey, Lynn. *The College Solution.* (Upper Saddle River, NJ: FT Press, 2008).

Resources for Students with Learning Disabilities and Attention Deficit Hyperactivity Disorder

Koehler, Michael. *Counseling Secondary Students with Leaning Disabilities.* (West Nyack, NY: Center for Applied Research in Education, 1998).

Kravets, Marybeth. *The New K & W Guide to Colleges for Students with Learning Disabilities.* (New York, NY: Princeton Review, 2007).

Lipkin, Midge. *The College Sourcebook for Students with Learning and Developmental Differences.* (Westford, MA: Wintergreen Orchard Press, 2009).

SAT Prep

Moshan, Michael. *Rock the SAT.* (New York, NY: McGraw-Hill, 2006).

The College Board, Princeton Review, or Stanley Kaplan test prep books.

Transition to College for Parents

Kasner, Laura and Jennifer Wyatt. *The Launching Years: Strategies for Parenting from Senior Year to College Life.* (New York, NY: Three Rivers Press, 2002).

Savage, Marjorie. *You're On Your Own (But I'm Here If You Need Me): Mentoring Your Child During the College Years.* (New York, NY: Fireside, 2003).

Online Resources

College Admission Profiles
Provides helpful information to college-bound students, school counselors, and college guidance specialists.
www.college-admission-profiles.com

College Board
Use the CollegeBoard.com's website to register for the College Scholarship Service Financial Aid Profile. The CSS Profile is the application used to apply for nonfederal financial aid.
www.collegeboard.com

College Confidential
Much of the information on CC is user-generated content. There are many official college admission office reps who participate along with other school counselors, teachers, and independent college consultants.
www.collegeconfidential.com

College Scholarships, Colleges, and Online Degrees
All-inclusive website that offers free scholarship searches.
www.college-scholarships.com

Cynthia Clumeck Muchnick, MA
Website for information on author's background and services as well as contact information to arrange a speaking engagement or workshop.
www.cynthiamuchnick.com

The Education Conservancy
A nonprofit organization committed to improving college admission processes for students, colleges, and high schools. EC provides advice, advocacy, and services.
www.educationconservancy.org

Enrichment Alley
Summer programs, school year enrichment, and gap year programs.
www.enrichmentalley.com

FastAid

A free online scholarship database. Also includes financial aid information and gives you help in understanding the SAR. The Student Aid Report (SAR) is the financial aid package offered by schools.

www.fastaid.com

FastWeb

A free scholarship search program where you can search for more than 1.3 million scholarships, student loans, financial aid, etc. Information on local and federal aid, a Q&A section, a financial aid timeline, and a glossary are also included.

www.fastweb.com

FinAid

Comprehensive free resource for objective and unbiased information, advice, and tools regarding financial aid, including a financial aid "calculator."

www.finaid.org

Financial Aid Assistance

All-inclusive website that offers financial aid advice.

www.financialaid4you.com

Free Application for Federal Student Aid

Online registration for the Free Application for Federal Student Aid along with answers to frequently asked questions about the financial aid process.

www.fafsa.ed.gov

Fresch Free Scholarship Search

Free scholarship search. Also covers financial aid, including a comparison of various loan programs. Special features include a section on scholarship scams and links to other sites of interest with a good description of each.

www.freschinfo.com

Guaranteed College Scholarships

Lists scholarships offered by specific colleges to students with a good combination of SAT scores and GPAs. The amount of the scholarships and the level of scores and grades needed to qualify vary widely.
www.guaranteed-scholarships.com

Independent Educational Consultant Association (IECA)

Listing of members of Independent Educational Consultant Association. Provides a pre-screened, legitimate college counselor search as well as pertinent articles and blogs.
www.iecaonline.com

Managing College Cost

Offers a complete understanding of the college financial aid/costs road map.
www.managingcollegecost.com

Modern Language Association

The go-to source for proper English grammar and usage.
www.mla.org

My College Options

Free college planning program.
www.mycollegeoptions.org

National Association of College Admissions Counseling (NACAC)

Useful website full of articles, resources, and current events pertaining to admission and college counseling fields, trends, and current events in general. Extensive LISTSERV open to members.
www.nacacnet.org

National Association for Fair and Open Testing

A nonprofit advocacy organization dedicated to preventing the misuse of standardized tests and offering a growing list of schools that are standardized test optional.
www.fairtest.org

Internet Resources for College Students

There are numerous fun and useful websites for college students. From buying textbooks to keeping in touch with family at home, there are resources on the Internet to help you with virtually any task or problem. Though you will certainly discover others during your college career, here are some Internet resources to give you a head start.

Academics

SparkNotes
A collection of study guides, including literary and nonliterary topics
www.sparknotes.com

Rate My Professor
Student ratings of professors at colleges around the country
www.ratemyprofessor.com

Cramster
Online homework help for many majors 24/7
www.cramster.com

Alternative Spring Break

Alternative Breaks
Many alternative spring break opportunities
www.alternativebreaks.org

Live United
Alternative spring break opportunities offered through the United Way charities
www.liveunited.org/takeaction/alternativespringbreak

Jewish National Fund
Alternative spring break trips for Jewish students
www.jnf.org/asb

Finding Dulcinea
This site provides a guide to alternative spring break programs around the world
www.findingdulcinea.com

Humor and Games

The Onion
A critically humorous news source
www.theonion.com

FARK.com
Obscure and unbelievable news stories
www.fark.com

Sporkle
Games, entertainment, and trivia
www.sporkle.com

StumbleUpon
A personalized browsing tool to help you find interesting websites
www.stumbleupon.com

Mini Clip
Online games site
www.miniclip.com

College Humor
Amusing pictures, movies, and games
www.collegehumor.com

Mad Blast
Movies, music, television and games that parody popular figures
www.madblast.com

JibJab
Political parodies and cartoons
www.jibjab.com

eBaum's World
"Media for the masses"—jokes, games, videos, and cartoons
www.ebaumsworld.com

HomestarRunner
Popular online cartoon
www.homestarrunner.com

Bored.com

Dedicated to procrastination and entertainment, with games, media, and links

www.bored.com

Milk and Cookies

Games and humorous news stories

www.milkandcookies.com

Darwin Awards

Honors those who improve the gene pool by removing themselves from it

www.darwinawards.com

Personal Space on the Web

Xanga.com

"The Weblog Community"

www.xanga.com

Livejournal

A site for online journals

www.livejournal.com

Angelfire

Provides free web space

www.angelfire.com

FreeWebs.com

"The next generation of free web hosting"

www.freewebs.com

Movies and Music

IMDB
The Internet movie database
www.imdb.com

Netflix
Movies for rent online
www.netflix.com

Sidereel
TV and Movies online
www.sidereel.com

OVG
Online video guide
www.ovguide.com

TV Duck
Free movies and TV online
www.tvduck.com

Hulu
Free movies and TV online
www.hulu.com

CMJ
"New music first"; music reviews, reports, and news
www.cmj.com

Pollstar
Popular music resource
www.pollstar.com

Allmusic
A place to explore new bands or genres
www.allmusic.com

Allmovie
Film and actor reviews and movie sales
www.allmovie.com

Textbooks

Amazon.com
Books, including new and used textbooks, and other products
www.amazon.com

Barnes and Noble
Books, including new and used textbooks, and other products
www.barnesandnoble.com

Half.com
An eBay partner site with new and used textbooks, as well as other products
www.half.ebay.com

efollett
Online location of a popular college bookstore
www.efollett.com

Bigwords
Helps students find the best deals on textbooks
www.bigwords.com

Chegg
Low-cost textbook rental site
www.chegg.com

Travel

Student Universe
A place to find cheap domestic and international flights, as well as resources for traveling in Europe
www.studentuniverse.com

Lastminute.com
A resource for travel within Europe
www.lastminute.com

EasyJet.com
Cheap travel within Europe and helpful to students studying abroad
www.easyjet.com

Expedia Travel
Flights, cruises, hotels, and travel packages
www.expedia.com

Orbitz Travel
Flights, cruises, hotels, and travel packages; Expedia competitor
www.orbitz.com

Southwest Airlines
Great prices if they travel to the vicinity of your destination
www.southwestairlines.com

Hostels Worldwide
Search over 25,000 hostels in more than 180 countries
www.hostelworld.com

Cheapo Air
The name says it all
www.cheapoair.com

E-Cards

All 4 Free
An Internet greeting card index
www.rats2u.com

Hallmark.com
The online site of the popular card and gift store
www.hallmark.com

Blue Mountain
Popular cards available to send online
www.bluemountain.com

Other Interesting Sites

Webshots
A place to post photos for friends and family
www.webshots.com

Facebook
An online directory connecting people through social networks at colleges and beyond
www.facebook.com

Campus Food
Online source for local restaurants that deliver
www.campusfood.com

Classmates.com
An online database of high school graduates
www.classmates.com

Doodle
Helps groups of people find shared availability for meetings, parties, etc.
www.doodle.com

Consumer Reports
A nonprofit organization and print magazine with product reviews and other information
www.consumerreports.org

Huffington Post
Breaking news and opinions
www.huffingtonpost.com

Notes

Notes

Index

We Have

EVERYTHING®

on Anything!

The Everything® list spans a wide range of subjects, with more than 500 titles covering 25 different categories:

Business	History	Reference
Careers	Home Improvement	Religion
Children's Storybooks	Everything Kids	Self-Help
Computers	Languages	Sports & Fitness
Cooking	Music	Travel
Crafts and Hobbies	New Age	Wedding
Education/Schools	Parenting	Writing
Games and Puzzles	Personal Finance	
Health	Pets	